Criminal Compliance – Concepts and Implementation

Luciano Anderson de Souza ·
Nathália Regina Pinto

Criminal Compliance – Concepts and Implementation

A Brazilian Perspective

Springer

Luciano Anderson de Souza
University of São Paulo
São Paulo, São Paulo, Brazil

Nathália Regina Pinto
University of São Paulo
São Paulo, São Paulo, Brazil

ISBN 978-3-032-15010-3 ISBN 978-3-032-15011-0 (eBook)
https://doi.org/10.1007/978-3-032-15011-0

Translation from the Portuguese language edition: "Criminal Compliance" by Luciano Anderson de Souza and Nathália Regina Pinto, © Authors 2019. Published by Thomson Reuters Revista dos Tribunais. All Rights Reserved.

The original submitted manuscript has been translated into English. The translation was done using artificial intelligence. A subsequent revision was performed by the author(s) to further refine the work and to ensure that the translation is appropriate concerning content and scientific correctness. It may, however, read stylistically different from a conventional translation.

This Springer imprint is published by the registered company Springer Nature Switzerland AG
The registered company address is: Gewerbestrasse 11, 6330 Cham, Switzerland

Preface

Compliance is a crucial topic not only in modern corporate dynamics, but also, particularly, for legal professionals of various specialisations, notably those focused on Criminal Law. This reality is indeed a watershed in the field of Economic Criminal Law, not yet fully understood in the Brazilian context.

To partially estimate the significance of this phenomenon, what can be considered the "*tip of the iceberg*", one only needs to think about the various corruption scandals that have erupted in recent years in Brazil, with particular emphasis on the "*Operation Car Wash*". From such cases, there has been a significant shift in corporate attitudes, both in terms of image and, fundamentally, in the construction (or reconstruction) of their structures, with compliance programmes taking a leading role as management and control coordination tools which, beyond a new corporate culture, pragmatically represent delimiters of corporate responsibilities.

In this vein, e.g., the following statement could be read in the press: "*Novonor is born as a holding company of a business group with 25,000 employees and six companies in the areas of engineering and construction, urban mobility and highways, oil and gas, real estate market, petrochemicals and naval industry*". Along with this text, the former Odebrecht, heavily impacted by the aforementioned *Car Wash*, published the commitments of the new company, Novonor, aimed at "*serving society through the operation of our companies, helping to build a sustainable future*".

Stigmatised by what became known as one of the biggest corporate scandals of all time in Latin America—which involved, in addition to Brazil, Argentina, Peru, Colombia, Mexico, Venezuela, Dominican Republic, Panama, Ecuador, and Guatemala—the former Odebrecht seeks to rebuild the history of a company founded in 1944 based on new standards of conduct and corporate governance. Both Odebrecht and the other cases cited in this work highlight the importance of effective *compliance* programmes that aim for much more than the minimum parameters determined by the regulations.

Frauds with real estate investments or with accounting balances, improper payments to public officials to avoid losses to activities or to secure future contracts, payments made by shell companies, frauds to mask environmental irregularities or even entire corporate areas dedicated to the administration of corruption practices are some examples brought in the analysis that clearly demonstrate the importance of *compliance* programmes for society as a whole.

The need to adhere to *compliance* programmes is primarily driven by American pressure for the prevention of international corruption crimes. However, today this threshold is greatly exceeded, shaping up as a powerful tool for preventing illicit activities, delimiting responsibility, and promoting positive values to corporate brands.

This work aims, therefore, to elucidate the challenges faced by corporations in their quest for internal controls that, more than just implementing models to prevent criminal irregularities, seek to develop ethical organisational cultures and business integrity.

Another point of attention that this analysis seeks to highlight is to ensure the character of *ultima ratio* of Criminal Law, so that its fundamental liberal principles are respected and attention (and care) is paid to its instrumentalised use, aimed at protecting market sentiments, and excessively expansive.

São Paulo, Brazil
January 2025

Luciano Anderson de Souza
Nathália Regina Pinto

Contents

About the Authors

Luciano Anderson de Souza Associate Professor of Criminal Law at the Law School of the University of São Paulo (USP). Tenured Professor, Doctor, Master, and Bachelor in Law by the Law School of USP. Postgraduate in Criminal Law by the University of Salamanca, Spain. Under the Springer publishing label, he is the author of *Economic Criminal Law: An Analysis from a Brazilian Perspective* (1st ed., 2025).

Nathália Regina Pinto Member of the Postdoctoral Programme at the Law School of the University of São Paulo (FDUSP). Doctor and Master in Criminal Law by FDUSP. Postgraduate in *Compliance* by the Getúlio Vargas Foundation (FGV) and Insper. Graduate from the Law School of Ribeirão Preto of the University of São Paulo (FDRP-USP). She attended a *Law Seminar* on the U.S. Legal System and the Constitution (*The U.S. Legal System and the Constitution*), at *Yale Law School*, and on Sustainable Capitalism and ESG at *Berkeley Law School.*

Chapter 1
What Is *Criminal Compliance*?

1.1 Contextualisation of *Compliance* in the Criminal Law Sphere

Before starting the analysis on *criminal compliance* and how it is incorporated into the Brazilian legal system, some brief notes on the role currently played by criminal law, especially in its economic aspect, are necessary. If previously criminal norms had the function of *ex post* regulation, that is, after the occurrence of a criminal irregularity, its current focus is on preventive conduct and practices, seeking to regulate and structure control barriers to the risks characteristic of business activity.

Since Criminal Law has an essentially political character, there is a trend for the legislator to act symbolically, transforming it into a tool of *combat* rather than legal protection of citizens against state punitive power.[1] This point requires greater attention when it is observed that the regulation of modern criminality will focus much more on risks than on damages—which may not even be produced.[2]

Furthermore, it is worth noting the existing concern with this discourse of *combat* widely disseminated today and Günther Jakobs' famous theory of Enemy Criminal Law. In a nutshell, for Jakobs, criminal law is chosen to confront dangers and, instead of waiting for the unwanted event to occur to provide a response, the treatment given to the *enemy*, the one who has ceased to be a citizen, will be prior, considering that, for the law, he will be seen as a *source of dangers* and not as an individual with rights and guarantees.[3]

Supplementary Information The online version contains supplementary material available at https://doi.org/10.1007/978-3-032-15011-0_1.

[1] Hassemer (1994, pp. 42–43).

[2] Hassemer (1994, p. 49).

[3] Jakobs and Cancio Meliá (2012, pp. 24–44).

L. A. d. Souza and N. R. Pinto, *Criminal Compliance – Concepts and Implementation*,
https://doi.org/10.1007/978-3-032-15011-0_1

In this sense, this work aims to highlight the importance of the preventive aspects of *compliance*, not understanding it as a *combat*, fight, or war against typical conduct, but simply a change of perspective and criminal policy, with a rationalising focus. There is indeed an ongoing reconfiguration of the organisational and functional architecture of corporations, but not to the detriment of the Democratic Rule of Law.

The world, as widely discussed in texts that seek to study the role played by Economic Criminal Law, is becoming increasingly complex. New technologies emerge without knowing their effects and risks, companies have grown in size until their turnovers have become more significant than entire National States and the resulting impression is that formal controls, hitherto used without much success, can no longer regulate the present and, much less, what is expected in the future.

In addition to colossal turnovers, the relevance of large corporations and financial conglomerates in regulatory systems is noticeable, considering the informational advantages and existing resources for risk management.[4] The social axis guided by Public Power gives way to the private sphere.

The weakening of States and the dissolution of geographical borders inevitably create sovereignty crises in countries whose legal systems are pressured for strategic regulatory alignment. As will be seen later, the integration of commercial activities pressures for a levelling of the rules and, in this influx, Criminal Law ends up gaining prominence as an alternative and strengthening of market regulations.

Globalisation is reflected from the reorganisation of notions of time and space, reducing distances to ensure the free circulation of the international flow of capital.[5] Large international organisations dictate the discourse to be followed by all, under penalty of economic sanctions that, in the face of financial integration, countries, especially from the Global South, have no interest (or capacity) in facing. The objective of institutions such as the International Monetary Fund (IMF), World Bank and World Trade Organisation (WTO), then, translates into the necessary creation of a *good business climate*", leading to a conduct alignment aimed at maintaining trust in the markets.[6]

In this vein, Anabela Rodrigues reflects on the relevance of the studies developed by the German sociologist Ulrich Beck, related to the insecurity characteristic of risk society, and compares them to what she calls a *new risk society*, a result of globalisation, in which we live in a permanent state of insecurity, without knowing for certain who those are that establish control relations in society.[7] What the author will characterise as a *mosaic* of different types of sanctions, increasingly rigid and longer, there is an increase in the role of Criminal Law, for example, from the expansion of the guarantor hypotheses, the creation of scapegoats within corporate structures (such as criminal liability *sliding* to the lower hierarchical layers) and by the use of

[4] Laufer (2006, p. 242).

[5] Harvey (2011, p. 22).

[6] Harvey (2011, pp. 63–86).

[7] Rodrigues (2017, pp. 159–163).

theories that increase the hypotheses of the use of criminal sanctions, such as the theory of willful blindness.[8]

In dealing with the expansion of Criminal Law, it will be a matter of the state's advance into the personal spheres of citizens, acting as a watchdog, ensuring policies aimed at prevention.[9] From the pressure exerted by various fronts that add to the complexity of modern societies, the need for a utopian Criminal Law that can control all (or at least, most) of the risks grows. The discussions then begin to consider the possibility of damage being caused in relation to the possibility that it actually occurs.[10]

It is interesting to note that the use of Criminal Law as a way to reinforce the economy did not arise recently. On the contrary, the so-called Economic Criminal Law has gone through some phases throughout history, such as (i) the case-by-case action in the periods of Antiquity and Middle Ages, when it was used as a way to regulate certain matters such as, for example, the establishment of the death penalty for those who forged coins in Ancient Greece; (ii) with industrialisation, where a systematisation of criminal norms aligned with the liberal state model emerges; (iii) subsequently, with the overcoming of the classic liberalism model, where there is a centralisation of state control, with special concern for the efforts aimed at the 1st and 2nd World Wars;[11] and finally, (iv) after the 1970s, with the economic crisis in the United States of America (USA) and consequent effects on the economies of other countries, policies aimed at reducing the role of the state regain space.[12] However, in this last phase, the increase in space for private agents and the development of new economic activities resulted in new points of attention for the state.[13]

What is observed, then, is that Criminal Law, oblivious to the economic reality, although intrinsically linked to the capitalist mode of production, will be used in an *emergency* manner, through normative constructions that are imprecise, ambiguous and whose completeness will only be obtained with the complement of other legal fields or even other areas of knowledge.[14]

In explaining the evolution of Criminal Law, Michael Kubiciel argues that the formulation of new typical conducts and their relationship with social complexity is not a simple matter, but a phenomenon that accompanies the dominant processes in political-criminal and economic terms.[15] For Kubiciel, changes in social structure demand the updating of Criminal Law, which cannot remain on the margins of the new reality while needing to establish limits for its use.

---

[8] Rodrigues (2017, pp. 163–164).

[9] Silva Sánchez (2013b, p. 165).

[10] Souza (2007, p. 119).

[11] Bechara (2008, p. 64).

[12] Souza and Araújo (2019, pp. 17–24).

[13] Bechara (2008, p. 64).

[14] Souza (2007, pp. 126 et seq).

[15] Kubiciel (2017, pp. 2–4).

In a reality where it is not certain which risks should be faced, criminal types stand out as a (supposed) option for protecting the institutions essential to society.[16] In search of a *Security State*,[17] criminal law is urgently required to regulate realities and risk contexts foreign to its liberal structure, with the purpose to give the impression that formal controls are effective.

Revisiting the idea that there is a demand for the harmonisation of rules that will regulate economic activity, what is observed in the current context is the prominent role played by private agents in the construction of this reality. As previously mentioned, the State, aware of its inability to regulate all economic activities, has been ceding space to corporations, within a logic of *regulated self-regulation*, in which public and private agents would work together in the development and implementation of regulatory policies.

It is in this influx that *compliance*, as well as its legal–penal aspect, emerges.

1.2 Notion of *Compliance* and Its Criminal Law Aspect

Compliance is synonymous with normative compliance, something more broad than simply legal compliance, as it also encompasses conformity to non-legal norms, that is, technical rules, as well as the principles of business ethics, promoters of corporate social responsibility.[18] *Compliance* is aimed at establishing risk management strategies, which are achieved through the so-called *compliance* programmes (*compliance programme*), that is, prevention models.

Within a neoliberal agenda and a movement of economisation of social aspects, marked by the search for efficiency in the role of the State, self-regulation gives *compliance* programmes the leading role in the so-called *regulatory capitalism.*[19] Its aim is to solve the problems of corporate irresponsibility and the possible damages caused to society as a whole, which is why it is required of the regulated to have their own prevention policies and internal data and information collection systems.[20]

In this sense, Nieto Martin defines *compliance* programmes as a "*tool available to management for controlling business activity*".[21] From a criminal perspective, *compliance*, now dubbed *criminal compliance*, aims to prevent the risks of crimes.

The *compliance* programmes, however, pose a challenge to Criminal Law as they represent a tool of business supervision often aimed at preventing liabilities and guided by *standards* of behaviour alien to the criminal reality, which need to be considered in the name of the effectiveness of efforts.[22] As will be seen throughout

---

[16] Kubiciel (2017, p. 6).

[17] Souza (2007, p. 156).

[18] Montaner Fernández (2020, p. 97 and following).

[19] Parker and Nielsen (2009, pp. 46–48).

[20] Parker and Nielsen (2009, pp. 60 and following).

[21] Nieto Martín (2019b, p. 34).

[22] Rotsch (2012, pp. 2–9).

this research, the economic notions of effectiveness and efficiency gain wide prominence in the development and implementation of criminal policies (when talking about the economisation of social aspects, this logic can also be brought to Criminal Law).

It should be emphasised that the reality of *compliance*, although not so recent in Criminal Law, when thinking, for example, already found space in the duties related to the prevention of money laundering in the financial sector. This construction developed in an administrative reality and not of *ultima ratio*.[23] Going further, one can notice the use of criminalisations as a tool for maintaining economic expectations and behaviours which seems to be incompatible with the structures of liberal Criminal Law.[24]

Moreover, in light of the above, it should be noted that in Brazil what has been observed is the overlap of protections. Beyond not respecting the character of criminal subsidiarity, there is a juxtaposition of legal regulation, with sanctions of different natures being applied for the same facts (in which the notorious example is corruption, which allows the application of the Brazilian Penal Code, the Anti-Corruption Law, and the Administrative Improbity Law).

The historical outline essential to the present analysis denotes that the beginning of the 2000s was marked by serious and significant frauds in companies that, until then, represented the solidity of the capitalist system. The scandals of Enron and WorldCom, for example, highlighted the importance of transparency measures and prevention policies that would aim to prevent ill-intentioned administrations from exposing the entire market to risk.[25]

Notorious scams such as the Enron and WorldCom cases were made possible due to the immense power of transnational corporations in the globalised economy. These American companies, as revealed in 2001 and 2002, were at the centre of two sensational financial scandals, involving billions of dollars in losses due to accounting fraud committed by their executives, aimed at artificially inflating their stock market value.

A common characteristic of both companies was that they took excessive risks in the name of economic growth (with an exclusive focus on policies that would yield returns for shareholders), and had centralised management that viewed the implemented compliance programmes and internal controls as a waste of time and investment.

The early 2000s were thus characterised by corporate greed, unprecedented frauds, widespread failures in the performance of gatekeepers and corporate governance

[23] Nieto Martín (2012, p. 124).

[24] Silveira (2020, p. 23).

[25] Roysen outlines how the scandals of Enron and WorldCom influenced the regulation of *compliance* practices and transparency duties following the publication of the *Sarbannes-Oxley Act* in 2002. Roysen (2003, pp. 192–213).

policies. As Laufer explains, such times favour the development of ineffective regulations, which are hastily approved "in the heat of the moment" without much deliberation.[26] This results in a "regulation game", where little is done to effectively prevent the same mistakes from recurring in the future.[27]

In this context, in 2002, the Sarbanes–Oxley Act (SOX) was enacted in the USA as a response to the frauds and widespread failures of the gatekeepers, here characterised as those responsible for certifying the information provided to the market. While it was seen as a strengthening of the rules related to corporate governance and mandatory compliance,[28] SOX faced criticism for merely reinforcing requirements already present in previous regulations and for the American legislator having toughened sanctions with the aim of regulating organisational practices through criminal law, thereby restoring investor confidence in the market[29] (thus, we witness the use of criminal law as a guarantor of the proper functioning of economic institutions).

Furthermore, critics pointed out that the limited discussions in the American Congress ignored studies indicating more effective auditing techniques, in terms of corporate governance, that could have been better utilised.[30]

Although SOX showed concern for the implementation of internal programmes that ensured the truthfulness of the information published to the market, a few years later we witnessed a new systemic problem with the use of financial instruments, the risks of which were allegedly little known even to the operators of large financial institutions, resulting in new stringent regulations. With the so-called subprime crisis in 2007 and 2008, subsequent to the historic financial bailouts and the corporations deemed too big to fail, the so-called animal spirits, and the total lack of risk analysis by financial institutions and investors regarding the real estate and securities assets held in their portfolios, the Dodd–Frank Act ("Dodd–Frank") was published in July 2010.

Dodd-Frank sought to fill existing gaps in the regulation of the financial system and revisit points that had already been the focus of SOX, such as transparency policies, risk analysis and prudential measures. One of the main highlights of the regulation was the protection given to whistleblowers, an important figure in the criminal policy of preventing corporate offences, as will be seen in the following sections of this paper.

It is possible to see that increasingly complex economic activities and the concern that they may pose excessive risks to society lead to the formulation of preventive measures to contain so-called criminally relevant dangers.[31] In practice, this refers to the control of risks from sources of danger as a sufficient justification for disregarding the ultima ratio principle of criminal law and, consequently, for its preventive action against harm to legal goods.

---

[26] Laufer (2006, pp. 239–240).

[27] Saad-Diniz (2019b, pp. 145–147).

[28] Nieto Martín (2019b, p. 32).

[29] Hefendehl (2004, p. 52).

[30] Laufer (2006, p. 241).

[31] Silveira (2006, p. 48).

Hefendehl highlights how the use of criminal law as *prima ratio* has gained prominence in the economic sphere due to more substantial changes related to organisational culture and new corporate governance practices.[32]

In this vein, in situations where the aim is to avoid conduct offensive to the economic order, the situations of danger will be outlined by the legislator, even if a necessarily harmful context is not identified at first.[33] The State seeks to protect supra-individual interests and those difficult to delimit, which allows us to identify, especially in Economic Criminal Law, two main characteristics of this expansion: its foundation in the idea of *security*, considering that the limits of corporate activities are increasingly complex, and the *symbolism* of the use of criminal norms, as a way to give quicker responses, but which are formulated without the proper academic-scientific debates and without the participation of specialists.[34]

The more serious the problem faced, the more legitimate the use of Criminal Law as *prima ratio* will seem, given that the new criminal types will be used in an *instrumental* way solely aimed at the "*symbolic preservation of the insecure risk society*".[35]

The use of criminal law as a guarantor of the feeling of trust is also perceived and, in this sense, it is demanded from the norms that they ensure the correct and regular functioning of the market.[36] Consequently, the economic criminal norm will seek to ensure that everyone follows the rules of the game, a goal that will be hard to achieve, as it will always be overtaken by reality.[37]

On this point, it is necessary to ponder the role played by enforcement agencies when applying the policies of *carrot and stick* (the logic of "*carrot and stick*", that is, of incentives and threats) and the challenge of its implementation, since, from the moment that the efforts of companies will be evaluated, it is necessary to establish criteria for this. Task forces and media mega-operations, as these policies are usually implemented, can have immediate effects but tend to be seen as isolated and without long-term effects, while the absence of effective measures can compromise the deterrent effect of the norm.[38]

Among the main challenges of the instrumental use of Criminal Law is the task of keeping up with dynamism, translated by the constant modification of corporate practices, and the large gap that separates it from the principles of legality and taxativity, fundamental in a Criminal Law of a liberal and guarantor nature.[39] Issues such as the difficulty of attributing responsibilities within corporate organisational charts and the popular appeal for large frauds not to be repeated influence the legislator to formulate open criminal types and blank criminal norms, whose complete sense will

32 Hefendehl (2004, p. 64 and following).

33 Silveira (2020, p. 142).

34 Silveira (2020, pp. 180–183).

35 Prittwitz (2003, pp. 262–263).

36 Souza (2012, p. 18).

37 Souza (2012, p. 65).

38 Laufer (2006, p. 244).

39 Souza (2019, p. 61).

only be possible if advised, or in some cases completely filled, by other branches of law (mainly administrative).

Furthermore, the preventive orientation of Economic Criminal Law will also be realised through omissive and negligent types, attributing to the subjects duties of care that are easier to typify, since it is not known exactly what is being protected nor the way in which the expected control will be obtained.

Rightly, Hassemer highlights that the reforms brought by globalisation permeate not only substantive criminal law, but also the criminal process, through the intensification of control instruments and the strengthening of agreements between the parties (*deals*) which, in the name of speed, disregard procedural formalities.[40] In the following chapters, it is intended to explain the use of these agreements by the State as a criminal policy aimed at efficiency, highlighting how the logic of the market has been influencing enforcement agencies and minimising the importance of individual and procedural guarantees.

Although economic crime has gained prominence in recent times, we must not forget the expressive selectivity characteristic of Criminal Law, which has the lower classes as its target audience. Thus, the Law must be thought of as a reality inserted within a certain society and, as Salvador Netto explains, "*Modern crime is the way in which contemporary society represents itself criminally*", with its control mechanisms and new legislative rationality.[41]

According to the author, while classical crime is tied to inequality and wealth, economic crime tends to be applied against those who control capital, and its regulation difficulties manifest themselves with the symbolism of norms, restrictive penalties of rights, and pecuniary fines.[42] As a result of this most recent expansion of criminal law, there is a hardening of norms that only worsens the situation of those who will face the system without the necessary legal support and the absence of prior planning on the criminal policy that is sought to be implemented in the country.[43]

If Laufer's criticism is considered, inequality, all things being equal, would also include corporations, given that large multinationals could have their sanctions mitigated if inserted within a logic of systemic risks,[44] while smaller companies are unlikely to be able to implement all the required controls. Here, we would witness the use of *compliance* programmes as a tool aimed at market domination and normative requirements.

According to Silva Sánchez's considerations, the so-called Corporate Criminal Law is guided by notions of maximum prevention and anticipation of the result.[45] Since the State has reduced its role as a service provider, it has had to strengthen

---

[40] Hassemer (2009, pp. 16–17).

[41] Salvador Netto (2008, pp. 144–145).

[42] Salvador Netto (2008, pp. 146–147).

[43] As Bechara asserts, it is difficult to verify coherence in the criminal policy implemented in Brazil, and one can speak of a "*crisis of legitimacy of Criminal Law in dealing with the criminality of the risk society*". Bechara (2008, p. 72).

[44] Laufer (2017, p. 112).

[45] Silva Sánchez (2003, p. 310).

its action in the preventive aspect, dividing its functions with private individuals through the establishment of so-called collaboration duties, seen as essential in the implementation of integrity and prevention programmes.

In this context, the State lost its centralising character as activities became specialised and the complexity and costs of performing regulatory, supervisory, and punitive functions became too high.[46] Thus, *compliance* is defined as the proper business organisation implemented with the aim of avoiding legally relevant risks.[47]

Silveira's differentiation can be highlighted, who understands that there would be two types of *compliance*, a more general one, aimed at the development of business management linked to the duties of implementing an *ideal conformity*, while *criminal compliance* would be aimed at *avoiding the violation of norms* and could be implemented, for example, through the provision of information required by anti-money laundering regulations.[48]

In this work, however, it will be assumed that *criminal compliance* constitutes one of the many prevention aspects that companies should consider when implementing their internal controls. That is, it has the strategic scope of managing risks of crimes.

Considering foreign experiences with the application of norms related to *compliance* practices, it is possible to perceive their close relationship with the criminal liability of legal entities, which, in Brazil, is only possible in the case of environmental crimes (Law No. 9.605/1998).

Analysing its characteristics, it is verified that, indeed, it is a regulatory reality aimed at requiring internal organisation from private agents. In Brazil, although the Anti-Corruption Law (Law No. 12.846/2013)—referenced below—has toughened, administratively and civilly, the punishments applied to corporations that do not have effective internal controls, in the criminal sphere the emphasis is given to the imputations of individual responsibility of the *guarantors*, for having failed to act as expected, which requires greater caution by the prosecuting bodies, under penalty of applying objective responsibilities in the criminal sphere, which is prohibited.

It is important to note that *enforcement* measures should not be seen as mechanical tasks, but the best alternative seems to be joint action between companies and regulatory bodies, through *voluntary compliance*.[49] Considering that the norms are unlikely to be able to cover all the constant innovations and, more than that, it proves to be an almost impossible challenge to ensure that companies can be in *compliance* in all the complex environments in which they operate. There need to be standards and *standards* for the application of the law, published in a clear and transparent manner.

---

[46] Coca Vila (2013, p. 44).

[47] Coca Vila (2013, p. 55).

[48] Silveira (2020, p. 26).

[49] Scholz (1984, pp. 387 et seq).

The so-called *cooperative enforcement* involves, in this context, regulatory bodies checking whether companies are implementing the minimum *compliance* requirements, bearing in mind that the procedures and regulations applied must be constantly updated to keep up with market developments.[50]

The fact that business activity has effects throughout the community makes the participation of all *stakeholders* crucial to ensure legitimacy of the controls implemented.[51] This point will influence the type of organisational culture implemented, whether effective or merely a *discourse of decorated words*, as Laufer asserts. For the author, the pro-social orientation begins with the hiring of employees, with fair incentives and remuneration and internal self-regulation, obtained from the participation of all interest groups.[52]

In summary, *compliance* programmes can be characterised as internal and continuous self-organisation efforts, which will be implemented through prophylactic measures of anticipation, detection and prevention of any criminal activity that may occur within the organisational structure.[53] What is advocated in this work is that, notwithstanding the importance of internal controls, an ethical corporate environment should be developed, in which all *stakeholders* involved with business activity participate.

It is hoped that the implementation of *compliance* programmes will effectively signify a change in corporate mentality and that regulatory frameworks represent more than a *hope*[54] or a *cloud of values*,[55] with companies having the duty of internal organisation. Going beyond concern with policies to *combat* irregularities, solutions should be sought that can break and, above all, overcome, the "*subculture of resistance, non-collaborative posture and non-compliance*".[56]

It is precisely the formation of a new attitude, with the internalisation of values, that will prove to be the most efficient means of preventing irregularities, mitigating the regulatory and repressive importance, including legal and criminal.

Finally, in conceptual terms, it is important to stress the distinction between *compliance*—usually translated in Brazil as conformity, despite the Anti-Corruption Law using integrity—and corporate governance. The *compliance* and corporate governance programmes, although similar, are not the same. While *corporate governance* is aimed at achieving general rules and behaviours for good business management, the *compliance* programme has a narrower objective, linking to the regular compliance with legal, technical, or ethical norms. Once again, both originate from Anglo-Saxon law.

---

50 Scholz (1984, p. 402).

51 Nieto Martín (2012, p. 125).

52 Laufer (2006, p. 245).

53 Wellner (2005, p. 500).

54 Salvador Netto (2008, p. 148).

55 Saad-Diniz (2019, p. 26).

56 Saad-Diniz (2019, p. 169).

Kuhlen[57] thus defines *compliance*: "*It is called* compliance *the measures by which companies intend to ensure that the rules in force for them and their members are complied with, that infractions are discovered and possibly sanctioned*".

Having presented this introduction, for internal controls to work, we will move on to analysing their pillars and most relevant points. However, a few words are necessary, as an introductory framework, to the Anti-Corruption Law, an essential guide to a Brazilian *compliance* programme.

1.3 The Brazilian Anti-Corruption Law and Corporate *Compliance* Programs

The phenomenon of corruption has been on the agenda for several years, in the legislative policy, on a global scale. The adoption of this discourse by political actors, media, Non-Governmental Organisations (NGOs), such as Transparency International, and multilateral entities, e.g., OECD, has led to an unprecedented level of punitive measures in this field.

Nevertheless, the adoption of a more appropriate criminal policy regarding corruption in the public sphere requires serious reflection on the administrative and civil mechanisms for curbing such practices. In the Brazilian case, it would be essential to focus on the analysis of the contours of the Administrative Improbability Law (Law No. 8.429/1992), as this law has proven to be the most significant extrapenal legal instrument on the subject since its enactment, deserving of improvement.

However, abstracting from this last observation, due to the international influx of coercion against corruption, coupled with local peculiarities, Brazil promulgated, on 1 August 2013, the so-called Anti-Corruption Law (Law No. 12.846/2013), aimed at civil and administrative accountability—primarily of legal entities, but not excluding individuals—for the practice of acts of corruption, broadly defined, as well as against tenders, to the detriment of national or foreign public administration.[58]

The acts harmful to national or foreign public administration are listed in Article 5 of the law, which establishes:

> **Art. 5º**
>
> Acts harmful to public administration, national or foreign, for the purposes of this Law, are all those committed by the legal entities mentioned in the sole paragraph of Art. 1º, which offend against national or foreign public

[57] Kuhlen (2013, p. 51 ([free translation]).

[58] On the subject, Silveira writes: "*In strict obedience to many OECD principles, and amidst a global policy of combating corruption, Brazil enacted Law 12.846/2013. It is quite interesting to perceive that it is not an explicit or necessarily criminal legislation but that, undeniably, it holds many institutes of declared criminal proximity*". Cf. Silveira (2015, p. 943).

> property, against principles of public administration or against international commitments assumed by Brazil, as defined:
>
> I - to promise, offer or give, directly or indirectly, undue advantage to a public agent, or to a third party related to him;
>
> II - provenly, to finance, fund, sponsor or in any way subsidise the practice of the illicit acts provided for in this Law;
>
> III - provenly, to use an interposed natural or legal person to hide or disguise their real interests or the identity of the beneficiaries of the acts committed;
>
> IV - with regard to tenders and contracts:
>
> a) to frustrate or defraud, by agreement, combination or any other expedient, the competitive character of a public tender procedure;
>
> b) to prevent, disturb or defraud the performance of any act of a public tender procedure;
>
> c) to remove or seek to remove a bidder, by means of fraud or offering of any kind of advantage;
>
> d) to defraud a public tender or contract arising from it;
>
> e) to create, fraudulently or irregularly, a legal entity to participate in a public tender or to enter into an administrative contract;
>
> f) to obtain undue advantage or benefit, fraudulently, from modifications or extensions of contracts entered into with the public administration, without authorisation in law, in the public tender call or in the respective contractual instruments; or
>
> g) to manipulate or defraud the economic-financial balance of contracts entered into with the public administration;
>
> V - to hinder the activity of investigation or inspection by bodies, entities or public agents, or to interfere in their performance, including within the scope of regulatory agencies and the inspection bodies of the national financial system. [...].

The highly repressive nature of the legal statute is highlighted by the establishment of *strict liability* for moral entities, as well as by the significant sanctions established. The punitive incisiveness is such that part of the doctrine understands it as criminal responsibility brought in fraud of labels.

In theoretical terms, an extrapenal discipline that respects the predicate of the *ultima ratio* by, apparently, renouncing in political-legislative terms the easy path of the tearing of the legal-criminal branch, ascertained in recent decades, would appear as something positive. In other words, the increase in non-penal mechanisms would be welcome with a view to constructing a more rational and effective regulation, instead of a simple escalation of penal recrudescence.

In this sense, the law under analysis would be per se commendable, were it not for the fact that, in the end, it overlaps with criminal protection and, more than that, also with other administrative ones, notably that relating to administrative improbity. This is without counting inherent difficulties of the law itself, which make the discipline of the subject even more questionable in the national reality. Let's see:

Preliminarily, it is observed that the Anti-Corruption Law promotes an overlap of responsibilities, generating a *bis in idem*, in view of the wording of its articles 3[59] and 30.[60] Therefore, for the same facts, both individuals and legal entities can be held accountable, not only under Law No. 12.846/2013, but also under the Administrative Misconduct Law or the Bidding Law, which seems inappropriate, as it is excessive.

Thus, the Anti-Corruption Law lacks fair interaction with other civil or administrative procedures, allowing double punishment for the same conduct in the non-criminal sphere.

Furthermore, it is important to note the lack of integration with the criminal sphere, which is symptomatically inferred from the discipline concerning leniency agreements.

Leniency agreement is a North American concept that involves an agreement between the legal entity that committed illegal acts and the authorities, in which the former commits to, among other measures, cooperate with the investigation of the facts, cease irregular practices, repair damages, and assume sanctions, in exchange for their mitigation (hence the name "*leniency*", understood as a punitive attenuation). Enshrined in the Anti-Corruption Law, this institute was already part of Brazilian antitrust legislation, having been studied for a long time by Competition Law.

Considered a pragmatic strategy for investigating corporate misconduct, based on the cooperation offered by the very person responsible for the illegal acts in a difficult context of determining materiality and authorship, the leniency agreement brought by the law in question deserves criticism for its own contours and also for the absence of provision for effects beyond its scope.

Thus, there are no advantages beyond the sanction mitigation procedure provided for by the law, which could potentially be a legal trap, given that there may be criminal liability for individuals or administrative misconduct for these and also for the legal entity itself. Regarding the latter case, however, it should be noted that the Anti-Crime Law (Law No. 13.964/2019) now expressly admits leniency agreements in cases of misconduct.

---

[59] "Art. 3º The liability of a legal entity does not exclude the individual responsibility of its directors or administrators, or of any natural person, author, co-author or participant in the unlawful act. § 1º The legal entity will be held accountable regardless of the individual liability of the natural persons referred to in the caput. § 2º The directors or administrators will only be held accountable for unlawful acts to the extent of their culpability".

[60] "Art. 30. The application of the sanctions provided for in this Law does not affect the liability processes and application of penalties resulting from: I - act of administrative improbity under the terms of Law n ° 8.429, of 2 June 1992; and II - unlawful acts covered by Law n ° 8.666, of 21 June 1993, or other public administration bidding and contract regulations, including those related to the Differentiated Public Contracting Regime - RDC established by Law n ° 12.462, of 4 August 2011".

In any case, a similar and expanded provision would be better, like the one existing in the current law that structures the Brazilian Competition Defence System (article 87[61] of Law No. 12.529/2011), where it is provided, in the criminal sphere, the suspension of the statute of limitations and the prevention of the offering of a complaint when a leniency agreement is signed, extinguishing the punishment once it is fulfilled. Thus, the Anti-Corruption Law could establish the same consequence for the criminal and also civil and administrative spheres, thereby encouraging the signing of said leniency agreements.

Furthermore, on this topic, the law reveals clear moralism by requiring that the leniency agreement results from the initiative of the legal entity (that is, according to article 16, § 1, item I, that "*the legal entity is the first to express its interest in cooperating for the investigation of the illegal act*"), something that the regulatory decree (Decree No. 8.420/2015), going beyond what the law establishes, illegally tries to cool down by establishing, in its article 30, item I, the expression "*when such circumstance is relevant*".

Despite understanding the requirement of spontaneity of the moral entity in triggering such an agreement, which in itself is already a pragmatic way of addressing illegality adopted by the legislator, it is illegal not to require it by infralegal rule when the law makes no exception. In other words, from *lege ferenda*, there should be a change in the latter; the regulatory decree cannot make an exception to it.

The discipline of the leniency agreement in the Anti-Corruption Law, in fact, abstracts to some extent the current international discussion of establishing *whistle-blowing* rules, lacking detailed—clear and secure—provisions on reporting channels and their consequences.[62]

There is merely generic mention in the law (article 7, item VIII[63]), providing for a case of punishment attenuation, little is specified in Decree No. 8.420/2015, which establishes that the integrity programs of companies should have as parameters, among others, "*channels for reporting irregularities, open and widely disseminated to employees and third parties, and mechanisms aimed at protecting good-faith whistleblowers*" (article 42, item X).

The absence of transparent and precise criteria to guide an efficient reporting mechanism compromises the effectiveness of the important measure. The assumption of illegality within the corporate context, most often composed of a multitude of

---

[61] "Art. 87. In crimes against the economic order, typified in Law n ° 8.137, of 27 December 1990, and in other crimes directly related to the practice of cartel, such as those typified in Law n ° 8.666, of 21 June 1993, and those typified in art. 288 of Decree-Law no. 2.848, of 7 December 1940 - Penal Code, the signing of a leniency agreement, under the terms of this Law, suspends the statute of limitations and prevents the filing of charges against the leniency beneficiary. Single paragraph. Once the leniency agreement is fulfilled by the agent, the punishability of the crimes referred to in the caput of this article is automatically extinguished".

[62] Saad-Diniz and Silveira (2015, p. 330).

[63] "Art. 7 º The following will be taken into account in the application of sanctions: [...] VIII - the existence of internal mechanisms and procedures for integrity, auditing and encouragement of reporting irregularities and the effective application of codes of ethics and conduct within the legal entity; [...]".

actors—partners or shareholders, managers, employees, and service providers—with a huge division of tasks, decision-making or even knowledge of all the nuances of facts perpetrated within it, is significantly complex.

A realistic law cannot simplistically, or even naively, consider that the authorities' pursuit of a leniency agreement due to a company's involvement in corruption offences is a simple and morally committed choice, moreover devoid of greater guarantees. Given that the focus of criminality comes from the company itself, not as a victim, the choice to assume guilt, in concrete reality, certainly arises from the tension caused by the action of repressive bodies, or by the imminence of their activation in the face of internal disagreements or disputes within the business context.

Therefore, more effective legislation must abstract from the spontaneity of expressing interest in cooperating to investigate the illicit act and, in addition, promote mechanisms of internal and external communication, in detail, with protective consequences[64]—such as, e.g., guarantee of confidentiality and job stability—provision for compensation for any losses suffered, exemption or mitigation of responsibilities, etc., since these mechanisms are relevant real drivers of the conclusion of leniency agreements or the punishment of those responsible for offences committed. This, in fact, is the Anglo-Saxon trend in the matter, which has led to the international expansion of reporting systems.[65]

The paradigmatic *whistleblowing*,[66] then, is aimed at establishing, within business structures, channels for complaints to be made, usually by employees, to a supervisory body, generally internal (as in the case of "*compliance officers*"), but also external, allowing the identification of offences in companies. This is a pragmatic strategy to prevent or suppress hotspots of criminality in these companies and, in this context, it is a sensitive way to generate leniency agreements or plea bargains, or, in the last resort, the appropriate punishments.

However, Law No. 12.846/2013 does not establish this hypothesis precisely, nor does it establish an interface between these last two figures, which are closely interconnected.

The assumption of responsibilities in the administrative sphere by the legal entity, generating mitigated sanctioning consequences, will often be made by the people responsible, to a greater or lesser extent, for the offences. For this reason, promoting this path, which ultimately aims to stop hotspots of criminality and impose punishments more effectively, quickly, and less costly to the State, implies the establishment, when there is interest from those involved, of the same type of conformity in the criminal sphere.

In this sense, there would be greater rationality in the combination of the institutes, in a unique way, with the participation of the executive body and the criminal prosecution body. Otherwise, a leniency agreement can, as asserted, be used for criminal repression, which will certainly inhibit its celebrations, contradicting the spirit of the law in a unique situation with correlated reflections.

---

[64] This according to the terms of the United Nations Convention against Corruption, 2003.

[65] Ragués I Vallès (2013, p. 94 and following).

[66] Ragués I Vallès (2013, p. 29 and following).

In other countries, where the criminal liability of the legal entity is more broadly in force than in Brazil, the criminal and extrapenal interrelation can be signalled as automatic, but this does not occur here, requiring specific discipline by national legislation.

Furthermore, the law under review, as well as its regulatory decree, is vague regarding *compliance* programmes, called integrity programmes.[67] Pointed out in the aforementioned article 7, paragraph VIII, also as a circumstance to be considered in the gradation of sanctions, nothing more is said about it in the federal law. The regulatory decree, in turn, in addition to rules of dosimetry[68] and the need for establishment in leniency agreements,[69] regulates the subject matter generically in its articles 41 and 42:

> **Art. 41**
>
> For the purposes of this Decree, an integrity programme consists, within the scope of a legal entity, of a set of internal integrity, audit and incentive mechanisms for reporting irregularities and the effective application of codes of ethics and conduct, policies and guidelines with the aim of detecting and remedying deviations, fraud, irregularities and illicit acts committed against the public administration, national or foreign.
>
> Single Paragraph. The integrity programme must be structured, applied and updated according to the current characteristics and risks of the activities of each legal entity, which in turn must ensure the constant improvement and adaptation of the said programme, aiming to guarantee its effectiveness.
>
> **Art. 42**
>
> For the purposes of the provisions in § 4º of art. 5º, the integrity programme will be evaluated, in terms of its existence and application, according to the following parameters:
>
> I - commitment of the corporation's senior management, including the boards, evidenced by visible and unequivocal support for the programme;
>
> II - standards of conduct, code of ethics, integrity policies and procedures applicable to all employees and administrators, regardless of position or function performed;
>
> III - standards of conduct, code of ethics and integrity policies extended, when necessary, to third parties, such as suppliers, service providers, intermediaries and associates;
>
> IV - periodic training on the integrity programme;

---

[67] Saad-Diniz and Silveira (2015, p. 335).

[68] Articles 5, § 4, and 18, item V.

[69] Article 37, item IV.

V - periodic risk analysis to make necessary adaptations to the integrity programme;

VI - accounting records that fully and accurately reflect the transactions of the corporation;

VII - internal controls that ensure the prompt preparation and reliability of the corporation's financial reports and statements;

VIII - specific procedures to prevent fraud and illegal activities in the context of tender processes, in the execution of administrative contracts or in any interaction with the public sector, even if mediated by third parties, such as tax payments, subject to inspections, or obtaining authorisations, licenses, permissions and certificates;

IX - independence, structure and authority of the internal body responsible for the application of the integrity programme and supervision of its compliance;

X - channels for reporting irregularities, open and widely publicised to employees and third parties, and mechanisms designed to protect good-faith whistleblowers;

XI - disciplinary measures in case of violation of the integrity programme;

XII - procedures that ensure the prompt interruption of irregularities or infractions detected and the timely remediation of the damages caused;

XIII - appropriate due diligence for the hiring and, as the case may be, supervision, of third parties, such as suppliers, service providers, intermediaries and associates;

XIV - verification, during merger, acquisition and corporate restructuring processes, of the commission of irregularities or illegal activities or the existence of vulnerabilities in the corporations involved;

XV - continuous monitoring of the integrity programme aimed at its improvement in the prevention, detection and combat of the harmful acts provided for in art. 5 º of Law n º 12.846, of 2013; and

XVI - transparency of the corporation regarding donations to candidates and political parties.

§ 1 º In the evaluation of the parameters referred to in this article, the size and specificities of the corporation, such as:

I - the number of employees and collaborators;

II - the complexity of the internal hierarchy and the number of departments, directorates or sectors;

III - the use of intermediary agents such as consultants or commercial representatives;

IV - the market sector in which it operates;

V - the countries in which it operates, directly or indirectly;

VI - the degree of interaction with the public sector and the importance of government authorisations, licenses and permissions in its operations;

VII - the number and location of the corporations that make up the economic group; and

VIII - the fact of being qualified as a microenterprise or small business.

§ 2 º The effectiveness of the integrity programme in relation to the harmful act under investigation will be considered for the purposes of the evaluation referred to in the caput.

§ 3 º In the evaluation of microenterprises and small businesses, the formalities of the parameters provided for in this article will be reduced, not specifically requiring, items III, V, IX, X, XIII, XIV and XV of the caput.

§ 4º It will be up to the Chief Minister of the Office of the Comptroller General of the Union to issue guidelines, rules and procedures complementary to the evaluation of the integrity programme referred to in this Chapter.

§ 5º The reduction of the evaluation parameters for microenterprises and small businesses referred to in § 3º may be the subject of regulation by a joint act of the Chief Minister of the Secretariat for Micro and Small Business and the Chief Minister of the Office of the Comptroller General of the Union.

The established parameters lack real concreteness, giving room for the establishment of merely bureaucratic compliance programmes.[70] In other words, the rules are overly broad, potentially resulting in programmes that merely reveal intentions, suitable for the simple aim of reducing punishment when applicable.

According to Silva Sánchez,[71] only the existence of an effective compliance programme has effects on the liability of both individuals and legal entities. Moreover, regarding the latter, adopted in a broad sense in Spain, unlike Brazil, it is important to note that, as the Spanish scholar[72] elaborates, it is more coherently compatible in a system that adopts it in conjunction with *compliance* rules. This is because it establishes a framework of permissible risk for the legal entity, which benefits in causal terms from individual behaviours understood as a neutral state of cooperation.

Despite the lack of broad compatibility of such ideas in the Brazilian case, it is understood that, even so, a business framework of this category mitigates or excludes

70 Noting that *compliance* programs, in order to fulfil their role in preventing offences, must be implemented under specific conditions and cannot merely be a *marketing* strategy, cf. Balcarce and Berruezo (2016, p. 159).

71 Silva Sánchez (2013a, p. 196).

72 Silva Sánchez (2013a, p. 37). In a similar sense, in Brazil, cf. Silveira (2015, p. 947).

individual responsibilities, both criminal and non-criminal, and can also have repercussions on the non-criminal expectation inherent to moral entities: as in the case of liability inscribed by the Anti-Corruption Law. However, this does not provide sufficient guidelines to allow the construction of a sufficiently secure theory.

There are numerous significant omissions in the regulation of the matter. There is a lack of establishment of clarification programmes, training and mandatory good practices for all employees, administrators and service providers with a view to preventing illegal acts.

The implementation of the programme by actors necessarily external to the company is not required, with some stability and broad autonomy—for example, being able to conduct investigations, demand the display of documents, and request the cancellation or non-signing of suspicious contracts—giving rise to integrity programmes, e.g., carried out by legal managers or other internal characters of the legal entity, without real independence, focus, and interest in the success of the task.

Furthermore, mandatory audits are not established with a certain frequency or in cases of mergers and acquisitions. Finally, the anonymity of complaints[73] or the job stability of whistleblowers is not guaranteed, as pointed out, thus not conforming to a harmonious and detailed discipline between *whistleblowing* and *compliance*: necessarily intertwined institutes, as correctly noted in national doctrine, Silveira.[74]

Another beneficial measure would be the provision of establishment of *compliance* programmes in the public sector, representing a reciprocity of treatment that would certainly contribute to the prevention of acts of corruption in this sphere.[75] In a socio-political context where the State has assumed a multitude of economic tasks, including violating Manichean paradigms, as referred to, there is no reason to exclude from the public machine the possibility of crime prevention in similar ways to the private initiative, this being a legitimate development agenda for Administrative Law in conjunction with Criminal Law.

Finally, in this illustrative list, it is noted that effective punishments for non-compliance with integrity programmes are not established. The laconic provision contained in article 42, clause XI, of the decree in focus, by simply raising the hypothesis of the need for "*disciplinary measures in case of violation of the integrity*

---

[73] Problematizing the issue, based on Spanish legislation, Ragués I Vallès observes: "(…) *it is perfectly possible that workers predisposed to report do not do so if they have to identify themselves, either for fear of reprisals or simply for not wanting to be seen as informers by their own colleagues. However, despite a system that admits anonymity may help overcome this fear, we must not forget that not having to reveal the identity of the whistleblower increases the risk of the reporting channel being used to make false accusations, although this danger can be avoided by requiring the anonymous whistleblower to provide some kind of evidence of their claims so that they can be considered plausible and give rise to an internal investigation*". Cf. Ragués I Vallès (2013, p. 181 [free translation]). Despite the risk of false reports, as warned by the professor from Barcelona, it is understood that anonymity is the best way to encourage reports, which, if false, will not result in liabilities.

[74] Silveira (2015, p. 946).

[75] Furthermore, there is an urgent need for legal restrictions on political appointments, to the detriment of technical criteria or public competition, in public capital companies, as well as in control bodies.

programme" allows, for example, the simple establishment of a formal warning as compliance with the requirement, which, in other words, paves the way for the execution of a farce.

Thus, among other measures, it could be established that the compulsory removal of members of the legal entity occurs in case of breach of the leniency agreement, or even forced sale of social participation in the same case.

The mechanisms of *compliance* are a reality in the current phase of economic globalisation, as seen, which is why their imposition by international agreements, or even by the pressure resulting from the trend towards extraterritoriality of Anglo-Saxon legislation (e.g., *FCPA*, *SOX* and *United Kingdom Bribery Act*) calls for the improvement of their acceptance with a view to risk management in the business sphere.

Beyond a legal obligation, moreover, their adoption often represents the restoration of trust in the market, which has objective reasons such as securing credits, ensuring the signing of contracts, increasing the price of shares, etc., in addition to avoiding more significant sanctions.[76] Despite being an ongoing reality, legal parameters are essential for its effective conformation.

Therefore, the effective adoption of mechanisms to prevent illegality in the business context, in this case with a view to curbing public corruption, whether national or foreign, in relation to the establishment of so-called integrity programmes, requires a more detailed and materially grounded conformation by Brazilian law. The current discipline lacks a greater substrate and, although recent, reveals itself as urgently in need of reform with a view to the implementation of a mechanism to more effectively curb serious illegalities that deteriorate the regular functioning of public functions.

1.4 Pillars of the Programmes of *Compliance* (Integrity, Ethics, Transparency and Prevention)

One of the essential characteristics of *compliance* programmes, forged from international anti-corruption conventions, is to delegate the task of crime prevention to the private sphere. In this influx, the safeguarding of corporate integrity entails the adoption of a series of appropriate regulations for this purpose, which is far from being a simple task.

According to Steinberg, "*without integrity, a compliance programme* will have form, but no substance, and over time will cease to do what it was designed to do".[77] This phrase is a good starting point for analysing the necessary pillars for the implementation of a truly effective *compliance* programme—not "*cosmetic*"—,

---

[76] This is notably evident with regard to construction companies involved in the "*Operation Car Wash*".

[77] Free translation of: "*without integrity, a compliance program will have form but not substance, and over time will fail to do what it's designed to do*", cf. Steinberg (2011, p. 33).

which aims to change the way companies do business and, as one of its fundamental purposes, prevent irregularities that can cause internal and external damage.

Implementing a *compliance* programme is not an easy task, but some fundamental pillars can initially guide efforts. Before referring to them, it is important to note that there is no pre-established formula for the necessary criteria for the implementation of an effective programme, since each economic sector has its risks and particularities (e.g., the pharmaceutical industry reveals particularities very different from those of an insurer or a bank).

More than that, knowing the format of the ideal programme proves to be one of the greatest challenges for those who, in some way, relate to the subject, whether in practice or in academic research. Consequently, knowing the reality of the business in question is essential.

State guidelines also fall short when it comes to the establishment of the minimum requirements that must be included in a *compliance* programme. This grey area proves to be very problematic in practice, as it can strengthen two undesirable paths: the symbolic use of internal controls and legal uncertainty in their evaluations, considering that the judges can carry negative preconceptions of internal controls.[78]

This, however, is the worst corporate scenario, as a *compliance* programme in such conditions represents a useless cost and, besides not preventing or mitigating the imposition of sanctions by the Public Power, at the limit, it can even mean its intensification, under the understanding that it is a farce orchestrated to mask illegalities.

The complexity of the issue increases if we consider the fact that regulatory policies tend to be oriented towards corporate guidelines, leaving it up to companies to define what will be considered an *ethical reference*.[79] If we think that *compliance* will be put into practice through formal internal controls that little, or nothing, will implement in terms of behavioural improvements, probably this model will not result in what is expected of it.

Nieto Martín rightly asserts that more important than a programme that seeks to regulate all business activity is one that can meet the basic control needs of the corporation.[80] From this perspective, it can be seen that the focus of *compliance* programmes will be solely on the prevention of irregularities. Although internal monitoring has its prominent role in the measures implemented, what is sought to be brought in this item is a perspective that *compliance* programmes should be, primarily, aimed at changes in culture (characterising the company as a good corporate citizen).

Understanding the context and the incentives that lead employees to commit improper conduct, for and in companies, has been the subject of intense research, and the complexity of the issue is reflected in the difficulty of specifying, after so much time, what the main causes are. Thus, the necessary integration with criminological studies needs to be highlighted.

---

[78] Nieto Martín (2012, p. 124).

[79] Saad-Diniz (2019, p. 14).

[80] Nieto Martín (2012, p. 124).

In the 1940s, Edwin H. Sutherland sought, through his research, to change the dominant criminological perspective that crime was always associated with social and economic vulnerability. Sutherland found that economic crime had certain characteristics that distanced the so-called *white-collar criminal* from the then more familiar street criminal (*street crime*), namely, (i) the *status* of a businessman; (ii) the distancing from punishments, including moral ones; and (iii) the low expressiveness of public commotion.[81]

The first point would involve the stereotype of the businessman, often associated with success and admiration in society, distancing himself from the classic figure of the delinquent. The distancing from punishments, in turn, could be explained by access to defence and the abandonment of physical suffering (the discussion of so-called *negotiated criminal law* will be brought up later) and, finally, the weak public commotion would be related to the technicality of irregular conduct and its diffuse effects.[82]

The difficulty in understanding the effects caused by corporate crimes could also be explained by the distancing of these activities and the sensationalism being, in the vast majority of cases, directed towards so-called violent crimes. In other words, such crimes would not be fully understood or would cause bewilderment in society.

In the theory formulated by Sutherland ("*differential association theory*"), criminal conduct, in the corporate sphere, would be a behaviour learnt associatively as a result of contact with an organisational culture oriented towards irregularities, which would be the result of a learning process of the maxim "*business is business*".[83] The illicit is normalised in that context.

In addition to the existence of a criminal culture within the company, internal and external factors could influence improper conduct by the components of a corporation. For Nieto Martín, contact with what he calls "*group criminal spirit*" and proximity to work colleagues, involved in improper practices, would be significant factors in deviant behaviour.

Add to this point the incentives considered problematic in companies such as, for example, bonuses focused exclusively on objective criteria, without considering the personal performance of the employee with the company's values, the existence of a competitive environment internally and externally (which would tend to vary according to the economic sector), and even the inherent characteristics of the capitalist system, which would demand from management a strategic direction focused on results.[84]

In addition to these points of attention, the way in which the flow of information develops within the company would also be determinant to ensure good management of internal activities, which would highlight the importance of internal information channels (ranging from direct lines to the deliberate blindness of managers).[85]

---

[81] Sutherland (2015, pp. 99–100).

[82] Sutherland (2015, pp. 102–104).

[83] Sutherland (2015, pp. 351 et seq).

[84] Nieto Martín (2019a, pp. 64–65).

[85] Nieto Martín (2019a, p. 67).

Other factors can also influence improper conduct in the development of corporate activities, from personal aspects of the agent to the organisational culture itself, which is why the challenge of setting up an effective *compliance* programme is so relevant to Economic Criminal Law.

More than being focused on punitive functions, internal controls need to integrate, harmoniously, their objectives of preventing irregularities with internal behaviour change, so that the culture of *acting correctly* perpetuates as if it were one of the assets of a corporation. As Saad-Diniz states, "*the importance of compliance programmes goes far beyond the simple defensive notion, its relevance lies in the development of strategies for improving business management*".[86] In other words, beyond profit, the aim is to avoid problems and[87] add market value to the corporation.

The way in which *compliance* programmes will be conducted will be detailed in Chap. 3, with the present item highlighting the fundamental points that should be considered. At first, therefore, the company needs to carry out due diligence to map the internal and external risks to which it is exposed (detection). In other words, knowing in detail the reality of the business and the challenges of the employees is essential.

The risks will be related to the activity carried out by the company, the regulatory environment in which it is situated, the number of employees, and the way they interact internally and externally on behalf of the company. Special attention should be given to the relationships maintained and contracts signed with public bodies. External payments also require constant attention from internal areas, whether by double approval criteria (four-eyes *policy*), alerts (*red flags*) highlighted according to the value of the payments and the parties involved.

In addition to detailing the risks they are exposed to, companies need to ensure that the *compliance* programme is proportionate to their characteristics, so that, it is reiterated, the implemented programme is truly effective and not a symbolic compliance with the norm. In this sense, proportionality and reasonableness should be taken into account both in internal application and by regulatory bodies in their assessments.

The aforementioned risk analysis cannot be conducted in a static manner, considering that economic dynamism demands constant and regular evaluations. The result may be the dissatisfaction of some areas that will interpret these efforts as opposing the efficiency and profits of the company.[88] The point of attention is to maintain the balance between the necessary internal controls and the development of an ethical organisational culture.

In this vein, Coca Vila establishes seven essential pillars for the effective implementation of *compliance* programmes, namely:

(i) the internalisation of a culture of compliance in which everyone understands the importance of the company operating in accordance with the legal system;

---

86 Saad-Diniz (2019, p. 128).

87 Veríssimo (2018, p. 91).

88 Bacigalupo (2008). Available at: https://www.elimparcial.es/noticia/26824/opinion/el-cumplimiento-del-derecho-como-valor-de-la-etica-y-la-cultura-empresarial.html.

(ii) the establishment of business objectives, through the setting of goals that must be achieved;
(iii) the carrying out of an inventory of the risks to which the company is exposed and the determination of ways to minimise these risks, bearing in mind that the total exclusion of risks is not possible or viable;
(iv) after mapping the risks of the company's activity, from a macro perspective, the micro-risks related to the activities carried out by the employees should be determined (at this point, the importance of training and adequate formation is highlighted);
(v) the delimitations of the positions of guarantee and responsibility within the business structure;
(vi) existence of internal communication systems that ensure the adequate flow of information within the company and, finally,
(vii) implementation of internal supervision and sanction systems.

Furthermore, it is important to emphasise that the models should be revisited periodically for the purpose of constant improvement. The *compliance* programme can never be static, since the very dynamics of business do not have this characteristic.

Linked to the latest ideas of ESG *(Environmental, Social and Governance)*, companies seek to add value that, although not new, has come to be seen as business assets. Practices that seek environmental sustainability, the development of socially positive activities, such as gender equality and, within the production chain, prohibition of the use of child labour are some of the examples that tend to enhance the internal organisation of a company. The same logic of *compliance* programmes applies to the implementation of ESG policies, under the risk of characterising the behaviours of *greenwashing* or *bluewashing* which, in general terms, represent the dissemination of false information to the market with the aim of portraying a reality of sustainability that, in practice, does not occur.

Given the above, the concept of *compliance* programmes can be divided into three stages, according to the division proposed by Saad-Diniz[89]: (i) a negative concept, when the objectives were limited to detecting, investigating and reacting to identified failures; (ii) a positive concept, characterised by internal behaviour aimed at good practices; and (iii) by the improvement of corporate governance strategies, risk management and *compliance* practices, evidencing a broadening of objectives, which went beyond the internal controls of risk mapping.

The challenge faced by *enforcement* bodies is to create evaluation parameters for the complex practices implemented by companies in each of their regulatory and economic contexts. The development of these criteria, which will determine the effectiveness of *compliance* programmes, corresponds to purely political–criminal decisions.[90]

In this influx, some examples of the work carried out by various legal systems are collated with the aim of clarifying more precisely what characteristics are expected from *compliance.*

---

[89] Saad-Diniz (2018, p. 47).

[90] Nieto Martín (2013, p. 33).

In Australia, in 2006, a standard known as *Compliance Standard* (AS-3806–2006) was published, which later gave rise to ISO 19.600, with the aim of clarifying concepts and determining the characteristics of *compliance* programmes that would allow internal controls to be classified as effective. Translating the standard, *compliance* is considered the fulfilment of requirements set out in laws, industry standards, organisational codes, principles of good governance, community and accepted ethical standards.[91]

This concept highlights the complexity involved in mapping all the rules that must be observed for the construction of corporate prevention measures. The culture of *compliance,* in turn, would involve the values, ethical parameters and convictions existing within the corporation and its interaction with internal structures and controls, in order to ensure that behaviours are aligned with good practices.[92]

AS-3806–2006 divides the most important points of a *compliance* programme into twelve principles divided into four major groups (commitment, implementation, monitoring, and continuous improvement).

The analysis of the principles allows us to glimpse practices that should be implemented by companies such as:

(i) participation of the entire executive body in the development, implementation and determination of improvements in the *compliance* programme;
(ii) need for clear and accessible language, as well as widespread communication of the standards throughout the company;
(iii) ensuring that internal policies are not isolated documents within organisational procedures, but integrated into them;
(iv) understanding how the activities carried out by the company are impacted by existing norms and *standards;*
(v) classifying the likelihood and consequences of potential failures in internal controls and how to respond to and implement improvements when identified;
(vi) determination of specific responsibilities of the *compliance* area, which is reflected in the job descriptions of those in charge;
(vii) recording of all activities carried out with the aim of implementing and ensuring the validity of internal standards, such as the training carried out;
(viii) making it clear that there will be no tolerance for behaviours that are not in accordance with prevention policies;
(ix) constant monitoring of potential weaknesses in the programme;
(x) encouraging the participation of all *stakeholders,* through formal or informal *feedback,* as a way of analysing whether the programme is robust and suitable for the objectives it proposes.

---

91 "1.3.3. Compliance - Adhering to the requirements of laws, industry and organisational standards and codes, principles of good governance and accepted community and ethical standards".

92 "1.3.4. Compliance culture - The values, ethics and beliefs that exist throughout an organisation and interact with the organization's structures and control systems to produce behavioral norms that are conducive to compliance outcomes".

Another interesting example is Chilean Law No. 20.393, of 2009, which established the possibility of holding legal entities accountable for irregularities committed in their interest and benefit.

One of the highlights of this law is the provision for certification of the efforts implemented by the legal entity: once the regulatory requirements are met, the company may have its *compliance* programme certified. However, the point of attention with regard to potential certifications is that they should not be thought of as *safe conducts* that allow the company to lose focus on monitoring and supervision.

In June 2020, the US Department of Justice (DOJ) published guidelines on the adequacy of *compliance* programmes and the mechanisms of internal controls implemented. Three questions were considered fundamental for companies to demonstrate that the programme is effective: (i) is the programme well designed? (ii) is the programme being seriously applied? and (iii) when put into practice, does the programme work?[93]

To answer these questions, the company needs to have more than a robust programme, but integrity policies that are sustainable and that are part of its daily life. For the DOJ, risk assessments to which the company is exposed involve everything from the location where its operations will be carried out, the sector of its activity, which directly impacts the applicable regulatory frameworks, as well as the business relationships maintained with customers, suppliers and third-party companies.

In addition to risk assessments, policies should be created that ensure the appreciation of the *compliance* measures implemented and aim to guarantee an adequate environment for their evolution, such as the existence of reporting mechanisms for irregularities, the engagement of senior management, and the allocation of sufficient resources and people, so that the *compliance* to present results and not merely serve as a front department. Training and communication policies are highlighted by the DOJ as essential for positive evaluations of the effectiveness of the *compliance* programme presented by the company to the regulator.

Recently, in May 2025, the DOJ published a memorandum known as the *White Collar Enforcement Plan* which sought to outline a direction for state prosecutorial action based on the principles of *focus, fairness, and efficiency.* While the head of the Criminal Division of the Department of Justice asserts that so-called white-collar crimes burden American businesses and harm national interests, he believes that state action should be carried out in a way that minimises burdens on corporations.

The guidance, as mentioned, highlights the role of efficiency and a concern with the possible impact of state action on the development of corporate innovations. A sensitive point raised is the representation of a strategic and geopolitical shift in treating Chinese companies as a risk factor for American investors and for internal anti-money laundering policies. In discussing fairness, the Criminal Division points out that the focus will be on the prosecution, civil and administrative, of individuals who would be, in the government's view, the actual perpetrators of crimes at the

[93] U.S. Department of Justice: *Evaluation of Corporate Compliance Programs*. Washington D.C, 1st of June, 2020.

expense of shareholders, workers, investors, and consumers. Regarding legal entities, the emphasis is on the necessary transparency of state expectations, so that an effective risk assessment can be made in corporate decision-making.

The memorandum mentioned other risk factors, such as the complexity of investigations carried out outside national territory, as well as the high costs related to the operation of independent *compliance* monitors, whose necessity should be evaluated on a case-by-case basis and thought out according to the positive returns that will be obtained, always considering the impacts that such interference can result in business activity.

The USA also has the *Sentencing Guidelines* which will provide some guidance on what is expected from *compliance* programmes. Section §8B2.1 ("*Effective Compliance and Ethics Program*") outlines, in general terms:

Section §8B2.1

(i) the importance of conducting *due diligence* to prevent and detect typical conduct in the organisation's activities;

(ii) promote an organisational culture that observes ethical conduct and that acts in accordance with the law;

(iii) the implementation of programmes that are suitable for the organisation's needs and that have sufficient internal procedures and controls;

(iv) constant supervision and evaluation of what has been put into practice, with a special focus on its effectiveness;

(v) individuals responsible for *compliance* must have sufficient resources and autonomy to address and report problems to the Board of Directors;

(vi) participation of senior management as a way to validate and ensure that the *compliance* programme is effective;

(vii) well-designed training that disseminates the intended organisational culture;

(viii) determination of disciplinary measures, when necessary and

(ix) periodic assessment of the risks to which the organisation is exposed.

The *Sentencing Guidelines* make it clear that the requirements for internal organisation are aimed at large and small organisations, with their responsible parties sizing the procedures and resources that are necessary for their reality.

In the capital market, the OCIE, that is, *Office of Compliance Inspections and Examinations*, of the *US Securities and Exchange Commission* (SEC),[94] values, in the evaluations made, that companies demonstrate the existence of routines of internal

[94] The SEC is the North American equivalent of the Brazilian Securities and Exchange Commission (CVM).

investigations that show that internal controls are not static, but are part of the day-to-day corporate administration.[95]

In this context, Philip Wellner expresses his concern about the bad incentives that may have gained prominence from the strengthening of the evaluation measures of the *Sentencing Guidelines* applied in the USA. In his view, instead of focusing on the development of an ethical culture in their activities, corporations tend to implement formal internal controls with the minimum required by the standard to be possible to decrease, or even exempt, responsibilities.[96]

According to this conception, the fact that the better the *compliance* programme, the greater the chances of discovering irregularities, may discourage private agents from implementing it. truly effective controls, as, within the raw reading of the law, such efficiency would not be required.[97]

According to Wellner, there would be four applicable guidelines for compliance *programmes*: (i) *compliance-based* (which would be the most encouraged by the *Sentencing Guidelines* and, therefore, more formalistic); (ii) *values-based* (on which there are studies demonstrating its greater effectiveness in preventing corporate irregularities); (iii) *external stakeholders*; and (iv) *top management protection.*[98]

The same criticism is presented by William Laufer when dealing with what he calls the "*compliance dilemma*", characterised by a game marked by disincentives that place companies within a choice in which, on one side, there are truly effective prevention and monitoring measures and, on the other, there would be regulatory lethargy.[99]

Within this game, then, there would be little or no ability to measure the effectiveness and authenticity of the implemented measures, as often, commitment is proven through numerous documents and evidence of training conducted instead of the demonstration of how internal controls positively influenced decisions made, internal planning, or even corporate culture.[100]

It also contributes to the difficulty of finding effectiveness parameters for compliance *programmes* that there are few effectively evaluated instruments, as cases of corporate crime are usually closed, as will be exposed *infra*, through negotiated agreements, with no published analyses on the strengths and weaknesses considered.[101]

Considering the specific character of each of the economic industries, there will hardly be a norm that provides a minimum standard of operation for all types of corporations.

Another trap to be considered is the reality of *overcompliance* which will focus on the appeal generated by *compliance* policies and result in imbalances within the

---

[95] Steinberg (2012, p. 5).

[96] In the same sense, in Spanish doctrine, Montaner Fernández (2020, p. 103).

[97] Wellner (2005, p. 505 and following).

[98] Wellner (2005, p. 513).

[99] Laufer (2017, p. 79).

[100] Laufer (2017, pp. 112 and following).

[101] Wellner (2005, p. 512).

market. In this influx, if implemented to meet only regulatory requirements, without concern for corporate behaviour, the effect will be the instrumentalisation of these measures, with little meaning in terms of ethics and much in competitiveness.[102]

It can be seen from the examples cited that States seek to conceptualise and establish minimum parameters of what should be part of compliance *programmes.* However, how can we know if all the efforts employed resulted in an effective programme? More than implementing various formal internal controls (the famous *window-dressing* programmes—façade), the main thing is that the system is suitable for the needs of the company in its entirety.

Therefore, one should avoid *compliance* programmes "*canned*" and that, in practice, are nothing more than a product traded on the market.[103] More than a cost or even a *necessary evil,*[104] compliance *programmes* should be seen as an element that is part of daily activities, naturally and not as something forced on its employees.

Therefore, much more efficient than an imposed guide of conduct, focused solely on formal norms, is the development of an appropriate culture integrated into the daily routine of companies.

References

Bacigalupo E (2008) El cumplimiento del derecho como valor de la ética y la cultura empresarial. El Imparcial, 10 de novembro. https://www.elimparcial.es/noticia/26824/opinion/el-cumplimiento-del-derecho-como-valor-de-la-etica-y-la-cultura-empresarial.html. Accessed on 11 November 2025.

Balcarce FI, Berruezo R (2016) Criminal compliance y personas juridicas. B de F, Montevideo-Buenos Aires

Bechara AELS (2008) Direito Penal e Economia: Tutela penal da Ordem Econômica. Revista da Faculdade de Direito de São Bernardo do Campo, year 12, n.14

Coca Vila I (2013) Programas de Cumplimiento como forma de autorregulación regulada? In: Silva Sánchez JM (dir.); Montaner Fernández R (coord.), Criminalidad de empresa y Compliance: Prevención y reacciones corporativas. Atelier, Barcelona

Harvey D (2011) O enigma do Capital e as crises do capitalismo. Boitempo, São Paulo

Hassemer W (1994) Perspectivas de uma moderna política criminal. Revista Brasileira De Ciências Criminais 2(8):41–51

Hassemer W (2009) El derecho penal en los tiempos de las modernas formas de criminalidad. In: Albrecht HJ et al (eds) Criminalidad, evolución del derecho penal y crítica al derecho penal en la actualidad. Del Puerto, Buenos Aires

Hefendehl R (2004) Enron, WorldCom and the consequences: business criminal law between doctrinal requirements and the hopes of crime policy. Buffalo Crim Law Rev 8(1):51–88

Jakobs G, Cancio M (2012) Direito Penal do Inimigo: Noções e Críticas, 6th edn. Lawyer's Bookstore, Porto Alegre

Kubiciel M (2017) Libertad, instituciones, delitos de peligro abstracto: ¿Un nuevo prototipo del Derecho penal económico? InDret—J Anal Law 3. https://raco.cat/index.php/InDret/article/view/328631

[102] Saad-Diniz (2019, pp. 89 and following).

[103] Laufer (2017, p. 115).

[104] Steinberg (2011, pp. 31–32).

Kuhlen L (2013) Cuestiones fundamentales de compliance y derecho penal. In: Kuhlen L, Montiel JP, Urbina Gimeno ÍO (eds) Compliance y teoria del derecho penal. Marcial Pons, Madrid
Laufer WS (2006) Illusions of compliance and governance. Corp Governance Int J Bus Soc 6(3):239–249
Laufer WS (2017) The missing account of progressive corporate criminal law. NY Univ J Law Bus 14:71–142
Montaner Fernández R (2020) Compliance. In: Silva Sánchez JM (dir) Lecciones de derecho penal economico y de la empresa. Atelier, Barcelona
Nieto Martín A (2012) Cosmetic use and lack of precision in compliance programs: any solution? EUCRIM, the Criminal Law Associations' Forum 3:124–127
Nieto Martín A (2013) Problemas fundamentales del cumplimiento normativo en el derecho penal. In: Kuhlen L, Montiel JP, Ortiz de Urbina Gimeno Í (eds) Compliance y teoria del derecho penal. Marcial Pons, Madrid
Nieto Martín A (2019a) Compliance, Criminologia e Responsabilidade penal da pessoa jurídica. In: Nieto Martín A et al. (Orgs.), Manual de cumprimento normativo e responsabilidade penal das pessoas jurídicas, 2nd edn. Tirant Lo Blanch, São Paulo, pp 62–122
Nieto Martín A (2019b) O cumprimento normativo. In: Nieto Martín A et al. (Orgs.), Manual de cumprimento normativo e responsabilidade penal das pessoas jurídicas, 2nd edn. Tirant Lo Blanch, São Paulo, pp 29–53
Parker C, Nielsen V (2009) The challenge of empirical research on business compliance in regulatory capitalism. Annu Rev Law Soc Sci 5(1):45–70
Prittwitz C (2003) Sociedad de riesgo y derecho penal. In: Arroyo Zapatero L, Neumann U, Nieto Martín A (coords.), Critica y justificacion del Derecho Penal en el cambio de siglo. Ediciones de la Universidad de Castilla–La Mancha, Cuenca
Ragués i Vallès R (2013) Los procedimentos internos de denuncia como medida de prevención de delitos en la empresa. In: Silva Sánchez JM (dir), Criminalidad de empresa y compliance. Atelier, Barcelona, pp 1–19
Rodrigues AM (2017) Controlar e Punir – o Direito Penal em mudança? Revista de Filosofia do Direito, do Estado e da Sociedade 8(2). https://revistafides.ufrn.br/index.php/br/article/view/324
Rotsch T (2012) Criminal compliance. InDret J Anal Law 1
Roysen J (2003) Histórico da criminalidade econômica. Revista Brasileira De Ciências Criminais 11:192–213
Saad-Diniz E (2018) Brasil v. Golias: os 30 anos da responsabilidade penal da pessoa jurídica e as novas tendências em compliance. Revista dos Tribunais, vol 988, ano 107, fevereiro de
Saad-Diniz E (2019a) Ética negocial e compliance: entre a educação executiva e a interpretação judicial. Thomson Reuters Brasil, São Paulo
Saad-Diniz E (2019b) Vitimologia Corporativa. Tirant lo Blanch, São Paulo
Saad-Diniz E (2019c) Compliance, Criminologia e Responsabilidade penal da pessoa jurídica. In: Nieto Martín A et al. (Orgs.), Manual de cumprimento normativo e responsabilidade penal das pessoas jurídicas. 2nd ed. Tirant Lo Blanch, São Paulo, pp 123–129
Saad-Diniz E, Silveira RDMJ (2015) Compliance, Direito Penal e Lei Anticorrupção. Saraiva, São Paulo
Salvador Netto AV (2008) Criminalidade moderna versus criminalidade de massa. In: Sá AA (coord) Criminologia e os problemas da atualidade. Atlas, São Paulo, pp 140–161
Scholz JT (1984) Voluntary compliance and regulatory enforcement. Law and policy
Silva Sánchez JM (2003) Libertad económica o fraudes punibles: riesgos penalmente relevantes e irrelevantes en la actividad económico-empresarial. Marcial Pons, Madrid
Silva Sánchez JM (2013a) Fundamentos del derecho penal de la empresa. Edisofer, Madrid
Silva Sánchez JM (2013b) A expansão do direito penal: aspectos da política criminal nas sociedades pós-industriais. 3rd ed. Revista dos Tribunais, São Paulo
Silveira RDMJ (2006) Direito penal econômico como direito penal de perigo. Revista dos Tribunais, São Paulo

Silveira RDMJ (2015) O Acordo de Leniência na Lei Anticorrupção. In: Badaró GH (org.), Doutrinas essenciais; Direito penal e processo penal, vol 4. Revista dos Tribunais, São Paulo, pp 157–177
Silveira RDMJ (2020) Direito Penal da era compliance, a realidade penal econômico-empresarial brasileira e a variação de seus momentos. In: Souza LA (coord.), Compliance no Direito Penal. Revista dos Tribunais, São Paulo
Souza LA (2007) Expansão do Direito Penal e Globalização. Quartier Latin, São Paulo
Souza LA (2012) Direito Penal Econômico: Fundamentos, Limites e Alternativas. Quartier Latin, São Paulo
Souza LA, Araújo MPC (2019) Direito Penal Econômico: Leis Penais Especiais. Thomson Reuters, São Paulo
Steinberg RM (2011) Governance, risk management and compliance: it can't happen to us—avoiding corporate disaster while driving success. Wiley, New Jersey
Steinberg RM (2012) The game changes: 10 essential elements for truly effective compliance programs. EDPACS 46(5):1–10
Sutherland EH (2015) Crime de colarinho branco: versão sem cortes, 1st edn. Revan Publishing, Rio de Janeiro
U.S. Department of Justice (2020) Evaluation of corporate compliance programs. Washington DC, 1 June
Veríssimo C (2018) Compliance: incentivo à adoção de medidas anticorrupção. Saraiva, São Paulo
Wellner PA (2005) Effective compliance programs and corporate criminal prosecutions. Cardozo L Rev 27:497

Chapter 2
How Do *Compliance* Programmes Appear in Regulatory Standards?

As mentioned, the organisational and procedural agenda of *compliance* programmes is broader than that of *criminal compliance*. The latter, among other peculiarities, has two regulatory frameworks that are already quite mature and detailed, that is, those related to the prevention of money laundering and corruption.

2.1 Regulatory Frameworks for Money Laundering Prevention

The regulatory understanding that seeks to prevent money laundering requires reference to an already sophisticated and significantly intertwined international context, in which Brazilian law is inserted. This is a joint effort by National States aware of the dissolution of geographical borders and the need for an orderly action in pursuit of greater effectiveness.

2.1.1 Context of Money Laundering Containment

International instruments, especially since the United Nations Convention against Illicit Traffic in Narcotic Drugs and Psychotropic Substances (Vienna Convention) of 1988, the first to establish a legal type of money laundering, formalised global concern with capital laundering and organised crime, as well as explored the first possible forms of criminal reactions to the phenomenon of money laundering.

Supplementary Information The online version contains supplementary material available at https://doi.org/10.1007/978-3-032-15011-0_2.

L. A. d. Souza and N. R. Pinto, *Criminal Compliance – Concepts and Implementation*,
https://doi.org/10.1007/978-3-032-15011-0_2

Globalisation and, consequently, the exchange of goods and capital, which, with the aid of new technologies, especially the *internet*, has gained a wider scope of operation.

Far from being static, the methods of recycling assets and values are constantly renewed and refined. The continuous improvement of the techniques used in its practice makes it difficult for the state machinery to identify and track the criminal movement, a situation that is exacerbated by digital communication.

This is opportunistic, reactive crime that ignores borders. As soon as the persecutory machinery, generally unprepared, identifies its stratagems, new deceptive devices and criminal structures are promptly created to conceal the illicit origin of money, assets, values, or capital.

Initially, the aim was to curb money laundering from drug trafficking through tax havens, using "*frontmen*", *offshores* and ghost companies, but, currently, increasingly complex and difficult-to-identify features are envisaged. The use of virtual space is mentioned, for example, through cryptocurrencies, which, being a more fluid environment, make it difficult to clearly ascertain placement, concealment, and integration, naturally breaking with issues of territoriality and extraterritoriality.[1]

Given the resilience of this type of crime, the lack of technique and specialised professionals to understand the chameleonic dynamics of the crime, there is a sequence of failures in curbing this problem.

Consequently, due to the state's wear and tear in dealing with it, simplistic strategies and mechanisms are proposed that do not always comply with legality and, fundamentally, open up space for arbitrariness. Duties, assignments, and surveillance obligations are also created for certain sensitive subjects, a role that should be performed by the persecutory bodies.

In the words of Silva Sánchez, it seems "*obvious that the legislative or jurisprudential creation of previously non-existent duty positions, or the expansion of existing ones, produces effects of responsibility expansion*".[2]

Obligated subjects are imposed police duties, turning them into forced collaborators of the State, they are considered as *gatekeepers* (watchtowers), in addition to serving as a containment barrier for the crime of money laundering, they approach the figure of the *whistleblower* by assuming the role of denouncers of crimes that they can (or should) identify.

This clearly shows the State's inability to prevent or investigate money laundering offences, using for this the forced collaboration of private institutions that operate in more sensitive sectors to the practice of this crime.

In this regard, if in the past, during the time of the first international conventions against money laundering, one could, at least in theory, rely on the application of the letter of the law and have an exact interpretation, as outlined by the legislator, currently, the effort is significantly greater in trying to anticipate any understanding *in malam partem*.

---

[1] Silveira (2018, p. 181).

[2] Silva Sánchez (2009, pp. 161–162).

The harmful effects of money laundering, which, alongside corruption crimes, undermine the democratic rule of law and destabilise the economic, financial and social order, are not denied; however, it is a cause for concern that the desire to curb these deviations by committing other irregularities in a maxim of distrust towards those who engage in lawful activities, but which can be used as instruments for money laundering.

Hence, it is not possible to deal with the possibilities of committing money laundering solely according to the text of the law, but, in parallel, one must take into account the dynamics of the punitive desire and the exhausted, perhaps defeated, look of the control bodies.

In Brazil, the criminalisation of money laundering gained ground with the promulgation of Law No. 9.613, of 03 March 1998, which deals with the crimes of laundering or concealment of assets, rights and values; the prevention of the use of the financial system for the illicit acts provided for in this Law and creates the Council for Control of Financial Activities (COAF), a Brazilian government agency responsible for preventing money laundering and terrorism financing once it shall receive and analyse reports of suspicious financial transactions sent from banks, brokerages and other reporting entities. COAF is the Brazilian financial intelligence unit (FIU), similar to the north-American FinCEN (Financial Crimes Enforcement Network).

The legislation is the result of international pressure to more rigorously curb economic crimes, such as money laundering and corruption, and was amended by the advent of Law No. 12.683, of 09 July 2012 ("*New Money Laundering Law*"), which had the clear objective of making the prosecution of money laundering crimes more efficient.

It is noted that in this legislation, as was the case on the international scene, there was a concern to incorporate administrative norms aimed at preventing recycling practices, with the clear objective of preventing money from crime from entering the financial system.

In this sense, the increase in control measures for suspicious operations stands out as one of the characteristics set by the "*New Money Laundering Law*", with the purpose of institutional improvement, through policies, procedures, internal controls, and communication with COAF.

COAF's purpose is to regulate, apply administrative penalties, receive, examine, and identify suspicious operations. Similarly, it is its responsibility to coordinate and create mechanisms for cooperation and exchange of information that enable quick actions.

Thus, one of the important aspects of the regulation is that it began to indicate who is subject to control mechanisms, that is, those who are obliged to identify customers and keep records, as well as report financial operations (article 11), establishing sanctions ranging from warning fines to the revocation or suspension of authorisation to carry out the activity, operation or functioning (article 12) in case of non-compliance with the legislation.

Money laundering (whitening or recycling) became known from the term used by the American press to report practices by mafia organisations to conceal values obtained from crime (*money laundering*).

Laundering is characterised by a complex structure that aims to give a lawful appearance to assets, rights, and values derived from any criminal offence. Traditionally, some of the main sources of illegal money are drug trafficking, currency evasion, smuggling, and corruption. It is noted that, by virtue of Brazilian Law No. 12.683/2012, the exhaustive list of crimes that precede laundering was abandoned, and any crime or misdemeanour can now figure in this antecedent to recycling.

This process includes the concealment (*placement*) and the disguise (*layering*) of the illicit origin, stratagems that serve as steps or stages to give a legitimate appearance to assets, rights or values derived from crime. These practices can take various forms, among others, through investments, acquisitions, and purchases of assets, culminating in recycling (*integration*).

These steps can develop in a divorced, simultaneous, overlapping, or chained manner and can be characterised as:

(a) *Placement*: the initial phase aimed at introducing illegally obtained values, that is, it aims to transform the illicit money derived from crime or misdemeanour into less visible values. In this way, bank transactions, the issuance of higher-value notes, the acquisition of high unit-value products, such as jewellery, precious stones and works of art, are symptomatic;
(b) *Layering*: the second phase of money laundering, also known as stratification or transformation. This stage is carried out by a succession of economic and financial operations, aiming to disguise the relationship between the money and its criminal origin, ensuring the anonymity of the author of the initial delinquency. For this, various businesses involving individuals and legal entities such as bank transfers, sending values to tax havens, investments in the stock market, etc. are carried out;
(c) *Integration:* In this third phase, legitimate goods and values, which now appear legitimate, are reintroduced into the economic and financial circuit through business and investments. Naturally, this phase is difficult to identify and prove, as the money laundering cycle is practically complete.

The repression of money laundering is not aimed at the exact preventability of the previous crime, but at the impossibility of the agent being able to benefit from the profit obtained with the preceding criminal conduct. Money laundering is a consequential crime, having a logical-formal link with the preceding offence and not a *post-delictum.*

Acts constituting money laundering behaviours are described and punished with imprisonment, from 3 (three) to 10 (ten) years, and a fine. The main figure provided for in the *caput* of Article 1, or in other words, to conceal or disguise the nature, origin, location, disposition, movement or ownership of goods, rights or values arising, directly or indirectly, from a criminal offence, as well as the equivalent figure consisting in the conduct of those who use, in economic or financial activity, goods, rights or values arising from a criminal offence.

2.1.2 Relevant Regulation in the Prevention of Money Laundering

In the regulatory frameworks related to the prevention of money laundering, discussions about the importance of internal controls and the implementation of *compliance* programmes are more consolidated and settled. Far from being a recent crime,[3] money laundering presents itself as a challenge to be overcome by regulatory bodies precisely because it involves identifying individuals within complex financial structures.

In their early generations, laundering policies aimed to determine which crimes would precede the need to camouflage the illicit origin of money and how the integration of National States should be conducted, in order to avoid the occurrence of unregulated spaces that would allow the flow of money without any type of supervision (as will be seen later, the integration of policies between countries will prove to be one of the biggest challenges in the prevention of money laundering). In the third phase, criminal policy essentially added the participation of private agents as collaborators of *enforcement* bodies.

In this influx, penal expansion developed in a context in which omissive conducts expanded and administrative obligations gave way to preventive penal types.[4] In the same vein, Silveira emphasises that Brazilian Law No. 9.613/1998 sought to stipulate "*the prevention of the use of the financial system for the illicit acts provided for*",[5] establishing the subjects who would be obliged to comply with the duties provided for and the administrative consequences to which they would be subject for failures in their internal controls.

Discussions about reducing or increasing regulation always have a captive space when dealing with economic activities. However, moments of crisis that affect society on a large scale cause this perspective to change, albeit temporarily.

The challenge is to develop strategic regulation that can minimise irregular conduct without harming or obstructing economic dynamism.[6]

In this context, the financial sector finds itself increasingly involved in prevention and detection policies for irregularities that, in some way, equip it to confer legitimacy on capital derived from more or less serious illicit conduct. The internal controls that will be required, as well as the prevention policies, will aim to increase the risks to the offender who will seek to integrate their gains into the economy.[7]

The path taken by regulation up to the enactment of Law No. 9.613/1998 was and continues to be quite long and winding. If banking secrecy rules date back to the time

---

[3] In a historical explanation, Liliya Gelemerova brings that the incidence of money laundering, albeit under another name, can already be observed in ancient Chinese merchants, who used various means to hide their capital from the government, or even the usurers of the Middle Ages and the pirates of the Mediterranean. Gelemerova (2009, p. 33).

[4] Saad-Diniz (2013a, b, p. 106).

[5] Silveira (2020, p. 31).

[6] Gill and Taylor (2004, p. 583).

[7] Blanco Cordero (2009, p. 119).

of the French Revolution, already in the 1920s of the twentieth century, discussions about the use of money derived from illicit practices gained prominence with the growth of organised crime and, later, intensified with economic development and globalisation post 1st and 2nd World Wars.[8]

In 1970, the *Bank Secrecy Act* was published, which can be characterised as the first anti-money laundering norm, although the concept was not yet fully materialised. By requiring financial institutions to keep records of transactions made, the norm aimed to regulate the concealment of illicit money.[9] It is worth noting that American law enforcement agencies regularly use this standard to soften allegations of money laundering liability, choosing to highlight the lack of internal controls in financial institutions rather than their use for money laundering.

The 1980s, in turn, were marked by the strengthening of the American war on drugs (*war on drugs*). At the time, the goal was to prevent drug traffickers from legitimising and, consequently, profiting from the money obtained from the illegal drug trade. This was a time of economic deregulation while criminal policies were becoming more stringent.[10]

For this, private agents, especially from the financial sector, were called upon to discuss the practices and controls that needed to be implemented to prevent money laundering. Their duty was to ensure business relationships only with good-faith clients, which could only be achieved with strict registration policies that, at first, were not well received by clients who valued confidentiality.[11]

In 1989, the *Financial Action Task Force* was created, known in Brazil as the International Financial Action Group (GAFI), an intergovernmental body responsible for assessing the context in which money laundering practices develop and developing preventive measures that must be implemented multilaterally.[12] After the attacks of September 11, 2001, initiatives against money laundering and terrorism financing became more severe, making demands for transparency and access to client information even more imperative.[13]

The mandate of GAFI then expanded to monitor the financing of terrorism around the world, intensifying after the terrorist attacks in Europe (Paris and Brussels) in 2015.

Understanding the path taken by money proved essential to prevent such serious acts of violence from being financed through the legal financial system. Later, with the case of the *Panama Papers*, the difficulty still faced by some countries in ensuring effective money laundering prevention measures was revealed.[14]

---

[8] Gelemerova (2009, p. 34).

[9] Gelemerova (2009, p. 35).

[10] Verhage (2008, p. 11).

[11] Gill and Taylor (2004, p. 586).

[12] Maillart (2020, p. 11).

[13] Verhage (2008, p. 13).

[14] Maillart (2020, pp. 13 and ff).

Through 40 Recommendations, which have been updated on several occasions as economic activities modernise, GAFI seeks to determine which points of attention should be observed by obligated entities. More than just recommendations, as the name might suggest, they are actually instruments used to pressure states to implement effective money-laundering prevention measures.[15]

If before the duties were related to the identification of organised criminal groups involved with drug trafficking, over time, they also began to address the concern with protecting the integrity of the financial system.[16] This is because it was realised that, even though there were changes in the structures of criminal organisations, the activity continued, which is why the focus should be on preventing illegal money from entering the formal economy, through *follow-the-money* policies.[17]

The regulation would then be applied within a sequence of behaviours that, seeking to give *an appearance of legality,* will mask the criminal origin of the money through fraudulent manoeuvres,[18] as previously explained.

Acting as the focal points of information related to money laundering, Financial Intelligence Units (FIUs) gained prominence in 1995 with the creation of the *Egmont Group*, aimed at international cooperation and the exchange of information across borders.[19] Today, they play central roles in the development of information-handling policies and the forwarding of indications of irregularities to the competent *enforcement* bodies.

The regulatory milestones for money laundering prevention have evolved with international discussion which, in 1988, with the Vienna Convention (Decree no. 154, of 26 June 1991[20]), highlighted that the signatory states were aware of the "*considerable revenues financial resources and large fortunes that allow transnational criminal organisations to infiltrate, contaminate and corrupt the structures of public administration, legitimate commercial and financial activities*", harming society as a whole. Its aim was, therefore, "*to deprive those engaged in illicit trafficking of the proceeds of their criminal activities and thus eliminate the main incentive for this activity*".

In the year 2000, through the Palermo Convention (Decree No. 5.015, of 12 March 2004), policies were established to promote cooperation in the prevention and combat of transnational organised crime. It would be up to each State Party to ensure the implementation of effective measures, from the investigation of suspicious conduct to the accountability of those who did not fulfil their roles within the monitoring structure.

---

[15] Gelemerova (2009, p. 36).

[16] Maillart (2020, p. 15).

[17] Badaró and Bottini (2013, p. 24).

[18] Oliveira (2019, pp. 65–70).

[19] Gelemerova (2009, p. 37).

[20] To contextualize, in Brazil, international treaties and conventions are not self-executing and must be incorporated into Brazilian domestic law through specific processes. Constitutionally, Congress must approve those treaties, as determined by article 49, I, and the President of Republic is responsible for ratify them (article 84, VIII of the Brazilian Federal Constitution). Without such promulgation, international treaties cannot produce domestic legal effects.

In 2003, finally, the Merida Convention (Decree No. 5.687, of 31 January 2006) highlighted the problem related to corruption and the need for recognition of multilateral instruments and the participation of the private sector with the establishment of internal controls and administrative duties of prevention.

In this context, there was an expansion of the obligations of private agents who began to have to collaborate with the State through three main duties: (i) the registration and recording of their clients; (ii) the reporting to the competent authorities of identified suspicious operations; and (iii) the development of policies of *compliance* and internal controls aimed at prevention and monitoring.

In Brazil, following the policies implemented around the world, the practice of money laundering can be described as the "*act or sequence of acts carried out to disguise the nature, origin, location, disposition, movement or ownership of assets, values and rights of criminal or contraventional origin*" which aims to reintegrate these values "*into the formal economy with the appearance of legality*".[21]

In summary, there are three classic verbs practiced in money laundering: concealment, dissimulation, and integration, which seek to distance the illicit origin of the money, making it difficult to trace its true source and introducing it into the economy in a legitimised way. It is important to note that Brazilian legislation does not require the process to go through all three phases to characterise the conduct as typical.[22]

If before there was a determined list of crimes and contraventions that could figure as antecedents to the practice of laundering, with the reform of 2012, it was determined that such provision would no longer be used. This made one of the points of attention with the norm of prevention of money laundering the lack of proportionality in equating both crimes and penal contraventions as preceding penal infractions.[23]

It can be highlighted that the duties of vigilance and collaboration demonstrate an orientation of criminal policy towards the anticipation of punishability of conduct and the prevention of irregularities.[24]

The first three paragraphs of Article 1 of Brazilian Law No. 9.613/1998 equate to money laundering the conduct of those who, in order to "*conceal or disguise the use of assets, rights or values resulting from a criminal offence*", convert them into lawful assets (paragraph I); acquire, receive, exchange, negotiate, give or receive as guarantee, keep in deposit, move or transfer (paragraph II) or import or export goods with values not corresponding to the true ones (paragraph III).

By performing these conducts, either alone or together, the subject will aim to remove the illegality of the assets, integrating them into his/her assets.[25] Regarding these paragraphs, it is necessary to highlight the necessary assistance with the concepts brought from Civil Law, and it is highlighted that part of the types constitute an excessive expansion of criminal protection, such as, for example,

[21] Badaró and Bottini (2013, p. 23).

[22] BADARÓ (2020, p. 137).

[23] Costa (2014, pp. 129–130).

[24] Saad-Diniz (2013a, b, pp. 9–10).

[25] Oliveira (2019, pp. 73 et seq).

when talking about keeping or having in deposit, which would not represent "*any form of transformation or concealment*", necessary for the configuration of money laundering.[26]

Paragraph 2 of Article 1 provides that the same penalty will be incurred by those who use "*in economic or financial activity, assets, rights or values resulting from a criminal offence*" (paragraph I) and those who participate "*in a group, association or office knowing that its main or secondary activity is directed at the practice of the crimes provided for*" in the Law (paragraph II).

As mentioned, the criminal policy of prevention of laundering has in private agents the main allies of the State. In this sense, Article 9 of the aforementioned statute outlines who the subjects are that need to observe the duties and conduct stipulated, with examples including financial institutions that perform activities of intermediation and application of financial resources, stock exchanges, insurance companies, real estate agencies, jewellers, commercial boards, and companies involved in the transportation and storage of valuables. These subjects will be required to keep their sources of danger under control, within the permitted limits.

Through the duties of information and collaboration required, it is evident that private actors play a significant role in surveillance and prevention policies. Article 10 of Law No. 9.613/1998, in turn, establishes the expected duties for the purposes of customer identification and record maintenance.

Among their duties will be the implementation of internal controls that allow the subjects to possess the information they may share with the State. In addition to identifying their customers through updated records (clause I), the subjects need to keep records of financial transactions carried out that exceed the limits set by the competent authority (clause II), as well as "*adopt policies, procedures and internal controls, compatible with their size and volume of operations*" (clause III).

The duties of collaboration are established by clause V, which determines that the agent must "*comply with the requests formulated by COAF in the periodicity, form and conditions established by it*", with the obliged subject preserving, when necessary, "*the confidentiality of the information provided*".

On this point, Resolution No. 4.753, of 26 September 2019, highlights the importance of procedures aimed at identifying and qualifying customers so that it is possible "*to appreciate, evaluate, characterise and classify the customer with the aim of knowing their risk profile and economic capacity*" (Article 2, §1).

It is the institution's duty to ensure that the documentation received is intact and authentic (Article 7, clause I) and, if there is irregularity in the information provided, the accounts should be closed (Article 6).

Antoinette Verhage divides into two the lines of supervision that should be implemented by the institutions: the first would be carried out by employees who, in their daily activities, maintain direct contact with customers and, thus, would be able to detect atypical operations from the analysis of criteria such as lack of economic basis; the second would be put into practice through supervision systems, parameterised to

---

[26] Oliveira (2019, p. 75).

know the routine of customer operations and, thus, be able to detect inconsistencies in them.[27]

In terms of the explanation provided by Oliveira, what can be highlighted is that it is required of the obliged agents to implement conduct (especially internal controls) effectively capable of preventing their financial institution, for example, from being responsible for creating what the author calls a "*state of affairs favourable to money laundering*".[28] Consequently, according to the risks faced by the obliged subjects, more or less intensified due diligence is required, ranging from *know your client* policies, through the monitoring of operations and transactions carried out, to direct contact with the client and dual authorisation controls.[29]

Starting with the first point, *know-your-client* policies require obliged subjects to carry out constant due diligence to keep all their customers' records properly updated. These measures can vary according to the risk exposure identified for each client, resulting in more simplified procedures being applied when the risk is lower and, otherwise, the measures applied should be intensified.

The duties of the agents begin with the first contacts of the client. By gaining knowledge about the classifying elements of a client, such as income, profession, investment objectives, the obliged subjects will be able to detect any irregularities, and identify operations that deviate from the expected standard, according to their established risk criteria.

At this point, the vulnerability of financial institutions in relation to the information and documentation received from their clients is highlighted. Presuming good faith, a characteristic of commercial relations, validating all and any data received becomes a thankless task, such as, e.g., the absence of a link with politically exposed people.[30]

In addition, the difficulty in defining concepts and objective standards of action can be highlighted.[31]

The sophistication of the methods used as procedures for money laundering demands, for certain clients, the need for reinforced due diligence procedures.

In situations that pose high risks, the private agent may require additional documentation about the origin of the funds, increase the number and frequency of implemented controls, request the economic rationale behind the transactions carried out, as well as identify involvement with politically exposed persons.[32] One of the greatest challenges for intermediaries and other obligated entities will be to distinguish between legitimate operations and those intended to conceal the criminal origin of the money.[33]

---

[27] Verhage (2008, pp. 17–18).

[28] Oliveira (2019, pp. 103–112).

[29] Oliveira and Cardoso (2020, p. 187).

[30] Gill and Taylor (2004, pp. 587 et seq).

[31] Gelemerova (2009, p. 41).

[32] Blanco Cordero (2019, pp. 549 et seq).

[33] Oliveira (2019, p. 25).

It will also be the duty of the financial institution to keep updated information and documentation of all analyses carried out, in case they are requested by regulatory bodies. More than that, proactive action is required to prevent irregularities: suspicious operations must be evaluated in advance and, if signs or proof of money laundering are identified, reported to the competent authorities.[34]

The quality of the information could be an indicator of the (lack of) quality of the internal controls implemented. The information must be kept by the obligated entities for a minimum period of five years, counted from the closure of the account linked to the client or the completion of the financial transaction carried out (article 10, § 2). However, it is important to note that the competent authority may extend this period.

While it is clear that there is a duty to identify clients and, with such information, carry out constant monitoring, it is less clear when the compiled data represents a *deal-breaker* or when they should be reported to the intelligence unit.[35]

The complexity of the duties to which the obligated entities are subjected has resulted in a reality called *de-risking*. As an example, Circular 3978/2020[36] provides, as a discretion of the financial institution, the evaluation of its interest in initiating or maintaining business relations with politically exposed persons (art. 19, §2, clause III). De-risking can thus be understood as the decision taken, for example, by financial institutions that choose not to accept the risks of maintaining business relationships with certain clients.[37]

Given the obligation to prevent the integration into the economy of capital derived from crimes and misdemeanours and the possible regulatory, financial, and reputational damages, the easiest solution seems to be to terminate the relationship with clients who may represent risks beyond those that the financial institution is willing to take.

It should be noted that the word "easy" is in quotes because this decision is anything but simple: considering the prohibition of informing clients about any investigations carried out, the termination of these business relationships tends to be a moment of doubt and questioning for both parties.

One could even argue that, considering the resources they have access to, financial institutions should seek balance and reasonableness before excluding a client.[38] In view of this context, it is proposed to use channels of contact administered by the Central Bank as a tool for resolving conflicts between banks and clients. These could

---

34 Blanco Cordero (2019, pp. 554–558).

35 Gelemerova (2009, p. 37).

36 Circular n.3978/2020 establishes a risk-based framework that drives the prudential supervision implemented by the Brazilian Central Bank in order to prevent money laundering and terrorism financing. It involves periodic risk assessments, realization of effective internal controls and corporate governance (including organizational culture).

37 Oliveira and Cardoso (2020, p. 181).

38 Oliveira and Cardoso (2020, p. 199).

question, in an appropriate forum, the measure taken by the institution which, in turn, could explain its reasons and, if applicable, cancel the exclusion.[39]

Continuing with the duties of the obligated entities, it can be seen that article 11 of Law No. 9.613/1998 determines the procedures to be observed to comply with the duty of communication. It is important to highlight that this article will be complemented by norms issued by different competent institutions, according to the activity carried out by the private agent.

The persons determined in article 9 of the diploma must communicate operations that present *serious indications* of money laundering crimes. On this point, it should be highlighted that private agents are not required to carry out exhaustive investigations of the indications identified, but at least to develop parameters and criteria for communication.

In this regard, the Securities and Exchange Commission (CVM) published, in July 2015, Circular Letter No. 05/2015/SIN/CVM with the aim of guiding participants on this duty of communication. In the document, the authority acknowledges the difficulty of the required monitoring, especially due to the complexity of the typical conduct that involves three distinct phases of action (placement, concealment, and integration) and explicitly states that it is not up to the obligated entity to be fully convinced of the illegality of the operation, as this analysis will be carried out by the Financial Intelligence Unit, the COAF.

However, in explaining the parameters of communication quality, the Securities and Exchange Commission of Brazil (CVM) establishes that reports should be individually crafted and detailed as thoroughly as possible. If the agent does not identify any unusual activity during the year, they should send a "*negative declaration*" to the regulator.

Also within the scope of the capital market, in August 2021, CVM Resolution No. 50 ("RCVM 50/202") came into effect, aiming to modernise and update the regulation regarding operations intermediated by participants. Based on four main verbs (*identify, analyse, understand,* and *mitigate*), the regulation requires market intermediaries to establish internal prevention and monitoring measures, in accordance with the risk appetite they have determined as a benchmark for their internal diligence.[40]

The resolution delegates a significant role to the senior management of financial institutions and, to make this possible, it stipulates that focal points should have broad and unrestricted access to all information flows within the company, as well as financial and technological resources that allow the implementation of effective internal controls.

Returning to Circular No. 3.978/2020, which provides for the policy, procedures and internal controls to be adopted by financial institutions in order to prevent the use of the financial system for money laundering or concealment of assets, rights, and values, there is a risk-based analysis,[41] from which institutions need to implement

[39] Oliveira and Cardoso (2020, p. 197).

[40] Pinto (2020, p. 167).

[41] Sheperd (2012, p. 11).

measures that are compatible with the risks identified to their customers, operations, products and intermediated services, and business relationships maintained with third parties. Its distinguishing feature is that the circular requires institutions to implement integrated policies to prevent money laundering, not just isolated measures.[42]

Among the provisions of Circular No. 3.978/2020, are the due diligence measures that should be put into practice by financial institutions regulated by the Central Bank, which involve everything from maintaining updated customer records, assessing risks related to products, new technologies and services provided, to developing an organisational culture and commitment to money laundering prevention policies, not only for internal employees, but also for contracted third parties. Specifically, the regulation stipulates:

> **Art. 2**
>
> The institutions mentioned in Art. 1 must implement and maintain a policy based on principles and guidelines aimed at preventing their use for money laundering and terrorist financing practices.
>
> Single paragraph. The policy referred to in the caput must be compatible with the risk profiles:
>
> I—of the customers;
>
> II—of the institution;
>
> III—of the operations, transactions, products, and services; and
>
> IV—of the employees, partners, and outsourced service providers.
>
> Art. 3 The policy referred to in Art. 2 must include, at least:
>
> I—the guidelines for:
>
> a) defining roles and responsibilities for complying with the obligations set out in this Circular;
>
> b) defining procedures aimed at evaluating and analysing new products and services, as well as the use of new technologies, considering the risk of money laundering and terrorist financing;
>
> c) internal risk assessment and effectiveness evaluation as referred to in Arts. 10 and 62;
>
> d) verifying compliance with the policy, procedures and internal controls set out in this Circular, as well as identifying and correcting any deficiencies found;
>
> e) promoting an organisational culture of prevention of money laundering and terrorist financing, including employees, partners, and outsourced service providers;

[42] Martinez (2020).

f) selecting and hiring employees and outsourced service providers, considering the risk of money laundering and terrorist financing; and

g) training employees on the subject of prevention of money laundering and terrorist financing, including employees of correspondents in the country who provide services on behalf of the institutions mentioned in Art. 1;

II—the guidelines for implementing procedures:

a) for collecting, verifying, validating, and updating registration information, aiming to know the customers, employees, partners, and outsourced service providers;

b) for recording operations and financial services;

c) for monitoring, selecting, and analysing suspicious operations and situations; and

d) for reporting operations to the Financial Activities Control Council (Coaf); and

III—the commitment of senior management to the effectiveness and the continuous improvement of the policy, procedures, and internal controls related to the prevention of money laundering and terrorism financing.

As stipulated in Article 9 of the circular under review, a focal point, a formally appointed director, should be designated as responsible for the implementation of the required internal controls.

Within their internal assessment, financial institutions must identify and measure the risk of their products and services being used in money laundering and terrorism financing (Art. 10) in a strategic and segmented manner. In areas where the risk is assessed as more significant, more robust controls should be implemented, whereas if the probability of risk is lower, the institution may use more simplified controls (Art. 10, § 3).

According to the circular, the policies of *know your client* will involve three phases: identification, qualification, and classification. In *identification*, the information to be obtained is related to basic registration data, such as name/corporate name, address/headquarters, and CPF/CNPJ (Article 16).

For *qualification*, procedures should be adopted that validate the compatibility of registration information with the client's risk profile, their financial capacity, the nature of the business relationship, as well as their status as a politically exposed person (Article 18).

The final phase involves the *classification* of clients according to criteria established by the financial institution in its initial risk analysis (Article 20). It is important to note that all phases should be continuously reviewed and updated. Finally, Article 23 of the circular prohibits the commencement of a business relationship with clients whose evaluations have not been completed.

With the aim of bringing the main improvements determined by the then-current CVM Instruction 617/2019, predecessor of the aforementioned RCVM 50/2021, the CVM published, in December 2020, the expectations of the autarchy regarding compliance with the duties established by the standard through Circular Letter No. 4/2020-CVM/SMI-SIN ("*Letter 4/2020*").[43]

In Letter 4/2020, the CVM explains that, based on the "*Risk-Based Approach*", obligated parties must "*identify, analyse and understand the risks of money laundering and terrorism financing*". Thus, the financial institution, within its risk parameters, determined for each type of client, should implement more or less robust measures to fulfil identification duties.

In the event of the impossibility of obtaining complete information about all its clients, the autarchy understands it is possible to start a business relationship, provided that the participant has the provision, within its internal policies, of this exceptionality. This aspect will involve enhanced client monitoring, a more careful analysis of the alerts generated by them, and the evaluation of the director responsible for ICVM 617/2019 on the maintenance of the commercial link between the parties.

Furthermore, the missing information should be collected "*diligently at the first opportunity and as a priority*". The regulation requires that participants define the frequency for updating their internal registers, which should be carried out at a maximum interval of five years for low-risk clients and, at most, two years for higher-risk clients. Although it was related to the now-updated instruction, Letter 4/2020 remains in force due to the relevant guidelines disclosed and considered by the market.

In this context, in addition to the *know your client* policies, the letter determines the necessary identification also of the ultimate beneficiaries of the intermediated operations. Whenever requested by the CVM or BSM Market Supervision ("*BSM*"), the participant will need to "*demonstrate that they have taken all reasonable measures within their reach to obtain complete identification of the client, including the ultimate beneficiary*".

As stipulated in Circular No. 3.978/2020, the financial institution must keep a record of all operations carried out, products and services contracted (Article 28). Regarding operations related to payments, receipts and transfers of resources, there must be identification of their origin and destination (Article 30).

Monitoring policies should be implemented based on the risk analysis conducted by the financial institution and pay attention to indications of money laundering, such as the lack of economic or legal basis for the operation carried out, the suspicion that the services provided constitute a device to circumvent internal controls, financial incompatibility of operations with the client's income, and the delicate relationship with politically exposed persons.

---

[43] Circular Letters represent a guidance issued by regulator (CVM) to regulated entities regarding specific regulations and how it must be observed by market participants. The circular letters are issued by CVM's technical departments.

Some believe that monitoring duties would be truly effective, given the difficulty, as mentioned, of validating the information received from clients.[44]

The CVM, on the other hand, highlighted in Letter 4/2020, that the regulator's expectation is that all transactions or situations involving the clients of the participants, especially in investment funds, are properly monitored, regardless of the value involved in the operation or the risk classification in which the client fits. Internal policies should provide a deadline for the analysis of situations identified atypicalities and, once the evaluation is completed, communication to COAF and CVM, if applicable, should be carried out within 24 hours.

It is important to mention that the regulation requires negative reporting, through which participants annually inform the CVM about the absence of suspicious situations or operations that should be reported to financial intelligence units.

Given all the regulations outlined in this section, we can summarise that there are three main areas of control measures required of those determined by the regulation: (i) the duties of identifying their clients; (ii) the duties of reporting to COAF; and (iii) the duties of internal organisation, which will be implemented through *compliance*[45] programmes. However, it should be noted that these are duties stipulated in an administrative regulation, and the lack of effective internal controls is not sufficient justification for attributing criminal liability to the directors and administrators of the obligated parties.[46]

These duties, therefore, highlight the aforementioned preventive nature of modern Penal Law, which requires constant vigilance from agents due to new responsibilities for action and information provision.[47] The use of repressive logic as a means of ensuring efficiency in criminal policy to prevent transnational crimes, which disregard borders and are becoming increasingly complex, can be observed.

The problem, however, is determining which measures work and whether there is, indeed, a deterrent effect of internal controls on those seeking to integrate illicit capital into the formal economy through financial institutions. The difficulty is even greater considering the limited capacity of intelligence agencies to analyse and forward suspicions that effectively constitute money laundering offences.[48]

The concern of regulators with technological innovations, such as transactions carried out through cryptocurrencies, which require constant updating of regulations (a concern reflected in Recommendation No. 15 of the FATF[49]), is highlighted.

---

[44] Gill and Taylor (2004, p. 592).

[45] Oliveira (2019, p. 229).

[46] Oliveira (2019, pp. 288 et seq).

[47] Silveira and Saad-Diniz (2013, pp. 250–253).

[48] Blanco Cordero (2009, pp. 126–129).

[49] "*Recommendation 15 - New technologies: Countries and financial institutions should identify and assess the risks of money laundering and terrorist financing that may arise in relation to (a) the development of new products and business practices, including new delivery mechanisms, and (b) the use of new or developing technologies for new or existing products. In the case of financial institutions, such risk assessment should occur before the launch of these new products, business practices or the use of new or developing technologies. Institutions should adopt appropriate measures to manage or mitigate such risks*".

On this subject, the CVM emphasises that participants should implement rules and internal procedures that allow for the handling of these new technologies, aiming to mitigate the risks related to money laundering, which demonstrates the open nature of the requirements and measures provided by *enforcement* bodies.

In this context, it is worth highlighting the growing concern of regulators, especially the Central Bank, with the use of new technologies, examples of which are *stablecoins*, which, in summary, are cryptocurrencies designed to maintain a stable value usually pegged to a specific reserve such as the dollar or euro. The use of *stablecoins* as a means of payment would pose an additional challenge to regulatory supervision and monitoring since the degree of traceability can be hindered by the type of *wallet* or *blockchain* used for cross-border payments.

Furthermore, in January 2022, Circular Letter/CVM/SMI/SNI/No.1/2022 was published with the aim of addressing the necessary sharing of information, for AML/CFT purposes, considering the operation of funds and investment portfolios based on the actions of their managers and fiduciary administrators. The central point of the letter establishes the legitimacy of data and information sharing—including about direct and indirect shareholders—among investment fund service providers and its harmonisation with the principles set out by Complementary Law 105/2001 and the LGPD.

Finally, there is one last diligence required of market participants that deserves mention, which is compliance with the prohibitions issued by OFAC (*Office of Foreign Assets Control), responsible* for publishing sanction lists, which must be observed by financial institutions, especially those that maintain any connection with the American financial system, representing another example of extraterritorial *enforcement* in terms of the FCPA.

This agency of the United States Treasury Department maintains updated lists of economic and commercial sanctions against individuals, organisations, and national states determined by the American government. The prohibitions range from institutions that finance China's military-industrial complex (as exemplified by Executive Order 13959) to the requirement to block financial assets held by individuals involved in serious human rights violations and corruption events (as exemplified by Executive Order 13818).

In this regard, it will be up to financial institutions to constantly monitor the restrictions issued by OFAC, considering also the possibility of applying significant sanctioning fines that can reach substantial amounts. In a recent case analysed by OFAC, the company GVA Capital Ltd. received the largest fine ever applied, amounting to US$215,988,868 for violating sanctions related to Ukraine–Russia by intermediating investment operations of a Russian oligarch, Suleiman Kerimov, despite being aware of his blockade. The operations involved the inflow of capital into the US and the purchase of shares in American companies and were allegedly executed through investment vehicles that could be known to be directly controlled by Kerimov.

From what has been seen in this section, the participation of private agents is crucial for obtaining information that allows regulatory bodies to analyse suspicious operations and implement an effective criminal policy that prevents the financial system from legitimising money derived from illicit conduct.

In this context, it is important to highlight the difficulty in knowing when the implemented measures are sufficient or when additional diligence is required to comply with the rules, without falling into the illusion that, in doubt, maximum controls are implemented for all clients. Firstly, because this would be highly costly for private agents and, secondly, because a higher number of notifications to intelligence units does not necessarily represent better *compliance* programmes.

2.2 Regulatory Frameworks for Corruption Prevention

Currently, the prominence of the regulation of *criminal compliance* is due to the international pursuit of curbing corruption.[50] Understanding this context is fundamental for assessing the current corporate legal detail.

2.2.1 Context of Curbing Corruption

There are two main contemporary sources of the constant legislative intensification in matters of corruption: one internal, represented by popular pressure led by the *mass media*, and another international, whose origin lies in international organisations and documents. Although with different origins, motivations and focuses, these two discourses meet in contemporary times, feeding each other.

This situation has led to a social recognition—true or not—of a possible "*systemic corruption*", which goes beyond the traditional contours of corruption as this or that type of crime protecting the functioning of the state machine against occasional harmful actions, to that of an international phenomenon capable of shaking economies and weakening the power of the nation-state in the face of organised crime.

Consequently, there is an international stance of "*global fight*" against corruption, understood to be confronted by a logic of "*combat*". Despite this trend having started, from the USA, in the context of unfolding investigations initiated shortly after the Watergate scandal[51] and, still under the aegis of the Cold War, also as a response to Soviet accusations of social degradation promoted by capitalism, facts that led to the promulgation of the *Foreign Corrupt Practices Act* (FCPA) in 1977, it is certain that at the end of the twentieth century and the beginning of the 21st, there is a significant radicalisation of its contours, mainly due to the economic tone of globalisation and its privatisation processes.

---

[50] According to Caro Coria, "*the privatization of the fight against corruption occurs through the figure of compliance*", cf. Caro Coria (2018, p. 110) (free translation).

[51] Koehler (2012, p. 932).

In other words, corruption is now an international issue and the shaping of *compliance* programmes aimed at its preventability is an inexorable reality and constantly expanding (including, since the FCPA, with claims of extraterritoriality[52]).

There is significant prominence of international pressure in the neo-criminalising framework around corruption in recent decades.[53] There are numerous regional and international documents from entities such as the Organisation for Economic Co-operation and Development (OECD), the United Nations (UN), the European Union (EU), the Council of Europe (CE), the African Union (AU) and the Organisation of American States (OAS), which have led to the penal expansionism observed in our legal–cultural environment.

Concretely, this has led to an understanding of the phenomenon as something beyond the state, that is, expanding the traditional understanding of corruption as referred to degradation in the public sphere. This is why crimes such as international corruption, private corruption, sports corruption, illicit enrichment, etc. are invoked. In addition to the harmonious intensification of primary criminalisation processes in internal orbits, efforts have been made to promote prevention instruments and international cooperation for investigation, punishment, and asset recovery.

At the initiative of the United States, the issue of curbing corruption was brought to the Latin American diplomatic agenda in 1994.[54] The growth of relations Chinese businesses, primarily in the traditional commercial sphere of influence of the USA, on one hand, and the strict control resulting from the application of the FCPA on American companies, on the other, has increased the dissatisfaction of political and economic agents in the latter country. They feel they are suffering negative consequences in trade, due to the corrupt actions of foreign competitors in this specific market, composed of developing nations with a significant history of tolerance towards acts of corruption.[55]

Thus, it was American pressure on the OAS that led, two years later, to the Inter-American Convention against Corruption, signed by thirty-four member states and not ratified only by Barbados, known as a "*banking paradise*". The convention, which came into force in March 1997, was the first international legal instrument on corruption. Its preamble specifically includes the recognition of the international negative impact of corruption and the need for the adoption of instruments to combat it, through international cooperation, with emphasis on extradition mechanisms, tracking and confiscation of assets, as well as assistance in obtaining evidence.

Next, the Convention on Combating Bribery of Foreign Public Officials in International Business Transactions, drafted by the OECD, was signed in December 1997, also after significant American pressure. This is because, until that time, the United

---

[52] Caro Coria (2018, p. 112).

[53] Despite being embryonically initiated by Resolution No. 3.514/1975, of the United Nations Organisation, regarding corruption in international commercial transactions, this movement was consolidated in the mid-1990s.

[54] Perla (2016). Available at: https://www.oecd.org/cleangovbiz/Integrity-Forum-16-Juan-Perla.pdf. Consulted on 15.02.2021.

[55] Perla (2016). Available at: https://heinonline.org/HOL/LandingPage?handle=hein.journals/rjnglbs16&div=9&id=&page = . Consulted on 11 November 2025.

States of America was the only country that criminally punished its citizens for the practice of corruption against foreign public officials.[56] For this reason, voices considered, as indicated, that they were in a position of inequality in the international commercial sphere, since economic agents from other countries could resort to corruption to conquer global markets.[57]

In the same vein, and expressly mentioning the actions carried out by the OECD, among other entities, the Criminal Law Convention on Corruption, of the Council of Europe, was approved in April 1999—after dialogues initiated in 1997 -, in the city of Strasbourg. In the preamble of this document, the same argumentative logic of the previously mentioned convention is already accepted, calling for international efforts to initiate a "*fight*" against corruption, seen as a detrimental practice to, among other social pillars, democracy, and free competition. This last mention signals the driving force for the adoption of economic agendas—moreover, delegitimising National States.

Still aiming at a standardisation of legislation and preventive and repressive measures at a universal level—that is, adopting a strategy of legal uniformity—and in view of the limited reach of the OECD, at the initiative of the USA, the UN began, in the same period, to embrace the discourse in favour of curbing corruption. Initially through efforts with the Office Against Drugs, shortly afterwards, in Palermo, in November 2000, the United Nations Convention against Transnational Organised Crime was organised, whose document expressly required its signatory countries to provide for the crimes of active and passive corruption of national public officials and suggested the same with regard to foreign officials.

Subsequent to this last convention, the UN General Assembly approved a specific resolution[58] regarding the need to develop an international legal instrument specifically aimed at the issue of corruption, which led to the Merida Convention in 2003. In addition to the aims of international cooperation for the prevention of corruption, the promotion of integrity programmes for the same purpose and the adoption of asset recovery measures, the highlighted international document explicitly—and emblematically—declares its aims to "*combat*" corruption, also using, in its article 1,[59] the expression "*fight against corruption*".

From this point on, the discourse of curbing corruption, as well as the respective national legislations, in our legal-cultural environment, aligns with this logic of penal strain. In the Brazilian case, the convention was incorporated into our internal legal system through Decree No. 5.687/2006.

As the most evident influence of this international political-criminal movement on Brazilian legislation, the provision was made in 2002, through Law No. 10.467,

---

[56] Perez Cepeda and Benito Sánchez (2013, p. 22).

[57] Perez Cepeda and Benito Sánchez (2013, p. 22).

[58] Resolution No. 55/61.

[59] "*Article 1. Purpose. The purpose of this Convention is: a) To promote and strengthen measures to prevent and combat corruption more effectively and efficiently; b) To promote, facilitate and support international cooperation and technical assistance in the prevention and fight against corruption, including the recovery of assets; c) To promote integrity, accountability and the proper management of public affairs and property*".

for the crimes of active corruption in international business transactions and influence peddling in international business transactions, among crimes against public administration. But the reach of the anti-corruption war rhetoric goes beyond this.

Alongside national peculiarities, it enhances a legislative discourse of hardening that also, e.g., led to the exacerbation of penalties in articles 317 and 333 of the Penal Code in 2003, or that initiated a series of legislative projects aimed at creating the crimes of private corruption and illicit enrichment, of inserting the corruption offences have been included in the list of heinous crimes, along with numerous measures, or "*packages*", to increase penal and procedural repression in matters of crimes against public administration.

In the face of the daily scandals exploited by the *mass media*, with constant new large-scale police operations, it is unlikely that the hardening stance on crimes against public administration will cool down in the near future in Brazil. Adding to this are international pressures led by American interests, signalling an increase in the repressive spectrum to predominantly private activities.

Ultimately, the issue of corruption has proven to be significantly complex, having been notable in recent decades for the exacerbation of punitive hardening. In the face of the distortion of criminal law resulting from this stance, accompanied by a social perception of minimal containment capacity, there is an urgent need to rethink preventive mechanisms, in addition to the dogmatic contours underlying the problem.

2.2.2 Relevant Regulation in Corruption Prevention

The end of the 70s was marked by a movement tied to moralism that emerged in the USA after the *Watergate* scandal, resulting from the Nixon government's funding by companies that did not declare these payments in their financial statements, as well as the subsequent discovery that about 400 American companies disbursed approximately US$300 million in illegal payments as a way to secure space in foreign markets.[60] The problem identified by the regulator was that companies saw these payments as a common practice, a necessity in terms of competitiveness and commercial issues.[61]

In order to prevent fraud committed by companies, especially in the arms industry, the *Defense Industry Initiative on Business Ethics and Conduct* was developed, which would later influence the creation of the *Sentencing Guidelines*, hence it could be argued that internal control measures were the result of self-regulation within the business environment.[62]

Adan Nieto contextualises the emergence of the FCPA, which he characterises as the "*seed of modern criminal policy*", with the decolonisation movements and the

---

[60] Bixby (2010, pp. 92–93).

[61] Fagali (2020, p. 33).

[62] Nieto Martín (2019, p. 33).

pursuit of development in former colonies. The need to develop countries, whose business structure was nascent, was widely exploited by large multinationals.[63]

The FCPA was then created with the aim of eliminating or at least reducing the use of bribes as a business practice, as well as giving special attention and transparency to the figures disclosed by companies. According to the legal text, corporations would need to avoid using bribe payments as an influence tool that could induce any type of illicit action, the aim of which was to secure business or ensure an undue advantage.[64]

The challenge faced by the US government was to balance the demands brought by the FCPA with the high competition in foreign markets. The solution was to ensure that the entire market was regulated by the same rules and that everyone was on the "*same page*" ("*levelling of the playing field*").

Businessmen, through the *lobby* carried out with the US government, used their power and political influence to ensure a normative system applicable to all those who were part of the market, both within and outside American borders,[65] which can be seen in the international requirements for all countries to have equivalent anti-corruption laws.

It is noticeable that supranational instruments, as well as measures related to money laundering, have a strong influence on the development of criminal policies that expand across all signatory countries of the various agreements signed.[66] One of the results of the pressure exerted by the USA was the OECD Convention on Combating Bribery of Foreign Public Officials in International Business Transactions, concluded in Paris in 1997, and incorporated into Brazilian law by Decree No. 3,678, of 30 November 2000.

Aware of an increasingly globalised international market, states realised the need for everyone to cooperate, taking the necessary measures to ensure the criminal prosecution of individuals involved in illicit practices or, in the case of legal entities, criminal or non-criminal sanctions, according to the legal system, that are effective.

Previously only aimed at US issuing companies, the FCPA gained a transnational character with the amendment approved in 1998, when it began to demand extra attention from companies and individuals ("any person") who maintained business relationships with American corporations, making it necessary to implement (and prove the effectiveness of) internal controls for prevention and procedures for internal sanctions of corrupt conduct.

In summary, the companies that are registered with the SEC (*issuers*), the *domestic concerns* which are businesses incorporated or headquartered in the US, the citizens, naturalised or residents in the US, and, finally, the *foreign nationals and entities* which will encompass all people who carry out illegal activities within American territory.

Designed with the aim of restoring confidence in US business, after the scandals of the 70s of the last century, the FCPA did not have significant application in its

[63] Nieto Martín (2013, p. 193).

[64] Bixby (2010, p. 94).

[65] Fagali (2020, p. 61).

[66] Barrilari (2020, p. 46).

first twenty-five years in force, gaining prominence from the twenty-first century with the increase in the volume of business and international investments, as well as multinational efforts to regulate and prevent practices related to corruption.[67] This point intensifies, particularly, with the economic growth of China and the high risk related to business conducted in the country, considering the high number of state-owned companies.[68]

Stephen Choi and Kevin Danis analysed the sanctions applied by the FCPA between 2004 and 2011 and reached interesting conclusions about the extraterritorial application of the rule. The authors' first hypothesis is related to legality, as the activity of *enforcement* will reflect the parameters and legislation agreed internationally.

Secondly, although there was a hypothesis that the US was seeking market development through corruption prevention regulation (the *altruism* hypothesis), in practice, what was found was a higher concentration of sanctions in developed countries and less *enforcement* with respect to American companies.

This confirmed the authors' third hypothesis (the *self-interest* hypothesis), which saw the FCPA as a tool for strengthening US interests and, finally, the fourth hypothesis was confirmed, that of *cooperation*, which highlighted the importance of coordinated action between countries, which favoured the DOJ and the SEC, who gained more access to evidence and, consequently, were able to structure more robust charges and secure convictions.[69]

With the strengthening of the application of the FCPA, another change was in relation to the dosimetry of the pecuniary sanctions applied, as it was determined that the restitution of the profits obtained by the offender should be included in the calculations.[70]

In a context where the focus becomes corporations and their internal organisations, *compliance* programmes need to ensure that corrupt measures are not used for favouritism or market conquest.

Effective *compliance* programmes will require constant assessments of corruption-related risks, demanding from those responsible to carry out monitoring, customised training (especially for those who maintain close contact with government agents from riskier countries), and to have updated protocols on how to proceed in the face of allegations or signs of irregularity in headquarters and branches around the world.[71]

It is important to note that there are three situations in which payment will not be considered a violation of the FCPA: (i) when it is legal in the country where it is made; (ii) when it is considered reasonable and in good faith; and, finally, (iii) the so-called *grease payments* which could be translated as "*facilitating payments*".[72]

---

[67] Reilly (2014, pp. 11–14).

[68] Bixby (2010, p. 117).

[69] Choi and Davis (2013, pp. 2–37).

[70] Bixby (2010, p. 109).

[71] Tarun (2011, pp. 58–60).

[72] Bixby (2010, p. 95).

This last item refers to amounts paid to mid-level officials with the aim of speeding up or ensuring that routine procedures are carried out and received various criticisms for the fact that the rule does not determine what value will be considered acceptable to the regulator. It has been agreed to consider the amount of US$1,000 determined by practice.[73]

Thus, it is important to highlight the subjective concepts that surround the practice of corruption under the terms of the FCPA.

The concern for the competitiveness of American companies, observed in the past, took on new dimensions in Trump's second term. On 10th February 2025, the president issued an executive order which determined that state action related to the FCPA would be paused with the aim of stimulating the economy and competitiveness of American companies, as well as national security.

Operationally, it fell to the Attorney General, *Pam Bondi,* to revisit ongoing investigations and *enforcement* actions and to release, as she deemed appropriate, *guidelines* and updated policies aimed at prioritising US interests. According to the document, the application of sanctions provided for by the FCPA was systematically harming American companies and citizens. As a result of the analysis, approximately half of the ongoing investigations were closed[74] and a new *guideline* was published.

In the Memorandum, published on 9th June 2025, some premises and limitations to the application of the FCPA were established, namely (i) the initiation of an investigation or *enforcement* action can only occur with the authorisation of senior department officials; (ii) the focus on strategies aimed at eliminating cartels and transnational criminal organisations that use corruption to facilitate their operations; (iii) the necessary analysis of the impact of certain payments on companies trying to gain a foothold in markets with characteristics different from those observed in the US (characterised as *"routine business practices in other nations"* or even *courtesies)*; (iv) focus on corrupt practices that could compromise institutions related to the country's infrastructure and, finally, (v) analyse the likelihood of a foreign regulator/ authority investigating and prosecuting the same conduct.

It is therefore noticeable, a weakening of state interest in its persecutory action in cases involving corrupt practices under the alleged justification that *enforcement* was harming American interests, even though there are few examples of American companies held accountable under the premises of the FCPA.[75]

Regarding the conduct of companies in this context of softening the FCPA, it should be considered that the guidance issued may not be the same in the event of a change in the Trump administration, coupled with the fact that other jurisdictions have maintained a focus on suppressing corrupt practices. In this sense, the expectation is that companies will not reduce their internal controls, nor will they downplay the seriousness of bribe payments in other jurisdictions given the regulatory complexity already faced and the compliance programmes already implemented.

---

[73] Bixby (2010, p. 110).

[74] Michaels and Fillion (2025).

[75] Sun (2025).

Returning to the relevant regulations published, the SOX also had a significant impact on the internal policies of corporations, as the American government was concerned with preventing the occurrence of new cases like Enron and WorldCom, which is why it began to require the disclosure of certified information to public bodies[76] and that companies conduct internal due diligence. As explained earlier, post-fraud contexts tend to be used as a lure for the implementation of stricter rules, not necessarily more effective ones.

A similar standard in its characteristics, the *UK Bribery Act*, the English law against corruption, can be cited, which determined the possibility of corporate criminal liability for failure in internal organisation. Like the FCPA, it has extraterritorial character, affecting any company that conducts (part of) its business in the United Kingdom.

Unlike the FCPA, the British anti-corruption version created four prohibited conducts: bribing, offering a bribe, bribing a foreign authority and failing, as a corporation, to prevent corruption.[77] The first two irregularities are related to the offering or solicitation of undue advantages for the performance of an activity that will be considered improper.

For the third prohibited action, a *close connection test* will be conducted to verify its jurisdiction and consequent legitimacy to act in the case. Citizens, residents, companies incorporated under the laws of the United Kingdom, or even Scottish associations will be considered as having a *close connection* and will therefore be bound by the Bribery Act.[78] The last, on the other hand, can be carried out inside or outside English territory, as it is applicable to companies that carry out all or part of their activities in the United Kingdom.

In addition to addressing private corruption, the regulation does not require the agent's intent, but considers it necessary for there to be improper conduct and, unlike the FCPA, does not provide exceptions such as *facilitating payments*.[79] Although it has created the criminal offence related to the lack of internal organisation, if the agent can prove the effectiveness and sufficiency of the controls implemented, they may avoid being criminally prosecuted by the *Serious Fraud Office* (SFO).

In 2010, the OECD produced a guidance document on best practices related to internal controls, ethics and *compliance* aimed at preventing and monitoring bribes to foreign officials.[80]

The document emphasises that the company should implement measures that are proportional to its needs, considering its size, type of activity, location, and operating sector. Going further, it highlights the importance of all employees, regardless of institutional hierarchy, receiving appropriate training on anti-corruption rules, whether the practices related to gifts, offering of accommodation, travel, political contributions, and donations, facilitating payments and extortion by public officials.

---

[76] Reilly (2014, p. 14).

[77] Hunter (2011–2012, p. 93).

[78] Hunter (2011–2012, pp. 95–96).

[79] Hunter (2011–2012, pp. 98–101).

[80] OECD: *Good Practice Guidance on Internal Controls, Ethics and Compliance,* 2010.

Such training should be properly documented, as seen in the case of Garth Peterson, and constantly updated.

In Spain, a country that had a strong doctrinal orientation against the criminal liability of legal entities, amendments were made to its Penal Code in 2010, in the famous article 31 *bis*,[81] which began to admit that "*legal entities will be criminally liable for crimes committed in their name, on their behalf or for their benefit, by their legal representatives and administrators,* de facto *or de jure*".[82] The importance of *compliance* programmes appears in paragraph 4[83] of the said article, which determines the mitigation of sanctions in case of the adoption of effective models of organisation and management.

In Brazil, with considerable delay, the aforementioned Law No. 12.846/2013 was enacted, which became known as the Anti-Corruption Law and provides for the objective liability, in the administrative and civil spheres, of legal entities that commit acts against the public administration, national or foreign. Although it is not a criminal law, it can be seen that there are certain characteristics within its structure that refer to this legal sphere, such as the logic of preventing irregularities, the high sanctions, which can lead to the closure of the company's activities, the difficulty faced by the defence, given the objective nature of the imputation of responsibility, the requirement of full cooperation with the elucidation of the facts, and also the concentration of powers in the hands of public bodies.[84]

As will be seen *infra*, the Madero case highlights, in a very didactic way, the objective nature of the liability of the legal entity, disregarding the context of the extortions committed by public officials, who offered undue advantages so as not to hinder the progress of the company's activities.

Similarly, for Bottini, understanding the severity of the law and the extent of its sanctions allows us to affirm that its interpretation must be done with caution and within the limits of the law, not allowing analogies that may, in some way, harm the defence of the accused, ensuring all procedural guarantees such as, for example, the right not to produce evidence against oneself.[85] For the author, cooperation with

---

[81] "*Article 31 bis. 1. In the cases provided for in this Code, legal entities will be criminally responsible: a) For crimes committed in their name or on their behalf, and for their direct or indirect benefit, by their legal representatives or by those who, acting individually or as members of an organ of the legal entity, are authorised to make decisions on behalf of the legal entity or hold organisational and control powers within it. b) For crimes committed, in the exercise of social activities and on behalf and for the direct or indirect benefit of them, by those who, being subject to the authority of the individuals mentioned in the previous paragraph, have been able to carry out the acts due to serious non-compliance by them with the duties of supervision, surveillance and control of their activity given the specific circumstances of the case*".

[82] Silveira and Saad-Diniz (2013, p. 101).

[83] "4. If the offence were committed by the individuals indicated in letter b) of paragraph 1, the legal entity will be exempt from liability if, before the commission of the offence, it has adopted and effectively implemented an organisation and management model that is suitable to prevent offences of the nature of the one that was committed or to significantly reduce the risk of its commission".

[84] Scaff and Silveira (2014).

[85] Bottini (2014).

public bodies should be a choice of the legal entity, and there should be no punishment for choosing not to produce evidence in a process in which the company is accused.

Regarding sanctions in the administrative sphere, which should take into account the specifics of the concrete case, the severity and nature of the infractions (article 6, §1), the fine will be applied in the amount of 0.1% to 20%, based on the gross revenue of the last fiscal year prior to the initiation of the administrative process, excluding taxes; however, it is not allowed to apply a fine whose value is "*less than the advantage gained, when its estimation is possible*" (article 6, paragraph I).

The convicted company will also have to publish the conviction decision in an extraordinary manner (article 6, paragraph II) for a minimum period of 30 days (article 6, §5).

The following factors will be considered for the application of sanctions (article 7): the severity of the offence; the benefit gained/intended by the offender; the (non) completion of the offence; the degree or danger of harm; the negative effect resulting from the offence; the economic situation of the offender; the cooperation of the legal entity with the investigations; the existence of internal integrity and audit procedures, as well as mechanisms to encourage the reporting of irregularities and the implementation of internal codes of ethics and conduct; and, finally, the value of the contracts signed between the offender and the injured public entity.

However, the law did not clarify what criteria would be used to assess the effectiveness of the internal controls implemented by legal entities, which only occurred, albeit timidly, later. Decree No. 8,240, of 18 March 2015, defined in its article 41, integrity programmes as:

> a set of mechanisms and internal procedures of integrity, audit, and encouragement to report irregularities and in the effective application of codes of ethics and conduct, policies, and guidelines with the aim of detecting and remedying deviations, frauds, irregularities, and illegal acts committed against the public administration, national or foreign.

Among the criteria that would be considered for the evaluation of the *compliance* programme implemented by the company, the decree highlights:

(i) commitment of senior management and their real support to the programme;
(ii) codes of ethics and conduct applicable to all employees and, if possible, to third parties linked to the company's activity (suppliers and service providers, for example);
(iii) periodic training;
(iv) periodic analysis of the risks related to the activity of the legal entity;
(v) ensure that the accounting records accurately and reliably reflect the company's financial information;
(vi) specific procedures to prevent fraud and illegal acts in agreements signed with public bodies;

(vii) independence and autonomy for those responsible for the implementation of the programmes and internal controls;
(viii) existence and disclosure of reporting channels;
(ix) provision of disciplinary measures;
(x) pre-established internal procedures to stop improper conduct and repair the damage caused;
(xi) conducting *due diligence* for the hiring of third parties and
(xii) continuous monitoring of the controls implemented.

In April 2015, Brazil's Office of the Comptroller General (CGU)[86] published, through Ordinance No. 909 ("*Ordinance 909/2015*"), guidelines on its evaluation of *compliance* programmes presented by legal entities and on how CGU will interpret and oversee their implementation. In order to conduct the evaluation, two types of report must be presented to the CGU: one on the company's profile and another on the conformity of the applied programme.

In the first report, the legal entity should indicate characteristics of its market, organisational information (such as, for example, number of employees, hierarchy, detailing of decision-making processes) and the type of relations maintained with the public sector, including the values of the contracts signed and the frequency of interactions carried out.

For the second document, the company must present which internal controls it had before the occurrence of the irregularity, demonstrating their operation, application routine (with historical data, statistics and concrete cases experienced), and how its programme acts in terms of prevention, detection, and remediation of harmful acts. The ordinance highlights that programmes implemented in a *merely formal* manner will not be considered for the purpose of reducing the sanction (which shows that a *compliance* programme, although expensive, is cheaper than a non-*compliance*[87]).

A recent case that exemplifies well the explanation we bring in this item involves Telefônica Brasil S.A. ("*Vivo*"). In 2019, after the CGU became aware of the agreement signed between the company and the *Securities and Exchange Commission* (SEC), in the amount of US$4,125,000.00, it requested clarifications to investigate a supposed irregularity involving the provision of tickets to seventeen public officials during the Confederations Cup in 2013, and at the FIFA Men's World Cup that took place in 2014 (Ordinance No. 2,047, of 21.6.2019).

Vivo did not deny the distribution of the tickets, but informed that it did so as an institutional action aimed at strengthening the brand. Furthermore, it argued that the agreement signed with the American body resulted from accounting problems, as it would have classified the tickets as advertising without specifying their distribution to public servants. Thus, according to the company's statement, there was no violation of the FCPA, only an irregularity in the balances presented.

---

[86] CGU is the federal government's internal control body responsible for activities related to the protection of public assets and the promotion of management transparency through public auditing, disciplinary oversight, anti-corruption prevention and enforcement.

[87] Gómez Tomillo (2016, p. 18).

Finally, in analogy to article 333 of the Penal Code, Vivo argued that the advantage obtained with the provision of the tickets, for which there would be no reason to attribute responsibility for any potential wrongdoing.

However, the CGU stated that Article 5, paragraph I, of the Anti-Corruption Law, which refers to the practice of "*promising, offering or giving, directly or indirectly, undue advantage to a public official, or to a third party related to him*" would be a formal illicit act, with the mere delivery, in this case, of tickets to a public official being sufficient. The federal agency highlighted the evidence present in the case, which included *emails* requesting the confidentiality of the names involved and messages that would justify the deliveries in exchange for "*continuous support to Telefónica*".

Considering the strict liability provided for in the law, it would be enough for the company to have sent the tickets for the irregularity to be characterised; however, more than that, the CGU stated that there were indications that the deliveries were directed to employees whose area of operation was related to Vivo's activity and that the company sought to maintain the advantages obtained with them. In addition, accommodation packages were also offered, amounting to approximately US$3,204.00, a value considered significant.

For the dosimetry of the sanction, the base calculation was the gross revenue of Vivo in 2018, with aggravating factors being the tolerance or knowledge of people from the executive body (high-ranking employees) and the contracts maintained with the involved public bodies. As mitigating factors, they reduced the company's penalty due to the fact that the advantages obtained with the tickets were not measurable, the collaboration with the investigations and the existence of internal controls.

It is important to note that when dealing with mitigating and aggravating factors, the federal agency extensively used the Penal Code as a source of analysis. The final sanction was in the amount of R$ 45,747,320.64 and the requirement for the extraordinary publication of the sanctioning administrative decision.

On 09 December 2024, Decree No. 12,304 was published with the aim of regulating the parameters and evaluation of integrity programmes in the event of contracting with the direct, autarchic, or foundational federal public administration for works, services, and supplies of great value (calculated according to the initial contract value and its eventual additions). For the company's integrity programme, which seeks the contract, to be considered effective, one of the points to be proven is, among other points, the ability *to prevent, detect and rectify deviations, frauds, irregularities, and harmful acts committed against the public administration, national or foreign* (art. 2, paragraph I).

As can be seen, the anti-corruption mechanisms to be implemented by private agents should take into account all the particularities involving possible relationships with internal and external public officials. With norms with extraterritorial applications, the supranational character and the logic of economic balance of the criminal policy of prevention of corrupt practices is evident.

References

Badaró JF (2020) Responsabilização penal pelo crime de lavagem de dinheiro a partir do descumprimento de deveres administrativos. In: Souza LA (coord) Compliance no Direito Penal. Revista dos Tribunais, São Paulo

Badaró GH, Bottini PC (2013) *Lavagem de dinheiro:* aspectos penais e processuais penais: comentários à Lei 9.613/1998, com as alterações da Lei 12.683/2012, 2nd ed. Revista dos Tribunais, São Paulo

Barrilari CC (2020) Passado e futuro da responsabilidade penal corporativa. In: Souza LA (coord) Compliance no Direito Penal. Revista dos Tribunais, São Paulo

Bixby MB (2010) The lion awakens: the foreign corrupt practices act—1977 to 2010. San Diego Int L J 12

Blanco C (2009) Eficacia del sistema de prevención del blanqueo de capitales: Estudio del cumplimiento normativo (compliance desde una perspectiva criminológica)

Blanco C (2019) A prevenção da lavagem de dinheiro. In: Nieto Martín A et al (orgs) Manual de cumprimento normativo e responsabilidade penal das pessoas jurídicas, 2nd ed. Tirant Lo Blanch, São Paulo, pp 527–581

Bottini PC (2014) A Lei Anticorrupção como lei penal encoberta. Consultor Juridico, 8 Jul

Caro Coria DC (2018) Compliance y corrupción. In: Calcina Hancco A (coord) Responsabilidad penal de las empresas y compliance program. Olejnik, Santiago de Chile

Choi SJ, Davis KE (2013) Foreign affairs and enforcement of the foreign corrupt practices Act. NYU Law and Economics Research Paper, No. 12–15

Costa HRL (2014) Os exageros e incoerências da nova Lei n. 12.683. In: Silveira RDMJ (coord) Crônicas franciscanas no Mensalão. Quartier Latin, São Paulo, pp 129–130

Fagali B (2020) A construção e consolidação do ambiente normativo global de combate à corrupção empresarial. Revista de Direito Penal Econômico e Compliance, Jan–Mar, pp 31–75

García-Moreno B (2020) *Del whistleblower al alertador:* la regulación europea de los canales de denúncia. Tirant Lo Blanch, Valencia

Gelemerova L (2009) On the frontline against money-laundering: the regulatory minefield. Crime L Soc Chan 52

Gill M, Taylor G (2004) Preventing money laundering or obstructing business? Bri J Criminol 44(4)

Gómez Tomillo M (2016) Compliance penal y politica legislativa: el deber personal y empresarial de evitar la comisión de ilícitos en el seno de las personas juridicas. Tirant lo Blanch, Valencia

Hunter SG (2011–2012) A comparative analysis of the Foreign Corrupt Practices Act and the UK Bribery Act, and the practical implications of both on international business. ILSA J Int Compar L 18

Koehler M (2012) The story of the foreign corrupt practices act. Ohio State L J 73:5

Maillart JB (2020) The anti-money laundering architecture of the FATF. In: Vogel B, Maillart JB (eds) National and international anti-money laundering law. Intersentia, UK

Martinez AAR (2020) Compliance Bancário e a nova Circular 3978 do Banco Central. Jota, 3 Nov

Michaels D, Fillion M (2025) Justice department resumes foreign-bribery work but cuts cases after Trump's pause. Wall Street Journal, 10 Jun

Near JP, Miceli MP (1985) Organizational dissidence: the case of whistleblowing. J Bus Ethics 4

Nieto Martín A (2019) O cumprimento normativo. In: Nieto Martín A, Garcia De La Galana B, Blanco Cordero I, Lascuarín Sanchez JA, Fernández Perez P, Saaddiniz E, Gomes, RM (orgs) Manual de cumprimento normativo e responsabilidade penal das pessoas jurídicas. 2nd edn. Tirant Lo Blanch, São Paulo, pp 29–53

Nieto Martín A (2013) La privatización de la lucha contra la corrupción. In: Arroyo Zapatero L, Nieto Martín A (dir) El derecho penal económico en la era compliance. Tirant Lo Blanch, Valencia

Oliveira ACC (2019) *Lavagem de dinheiro:* responsabilidade pela omissão de informações. Tirant Lo Blanch, São Paulo

Oliveira ACC, Cardoso DM (2020) De-risking: parâmetros para medidas de diligência nos programas de compliance das instituições financeiras. In: Souza LA (coord) Compliance no Direito Penal. Revista dos Tribunais, São Paulo

Perez Cepeda AI, Benito Sánchez D (2013) La Politica criminal internacional contra la corrupción. In: Berdugo Gómez de la Torre I, Bechara AELS (coords) Estudios sobre la corrupción: una reflexión hispano brasileña. Centro de Estudios Brasileños, Salamanca, p 22

Perla JO (2016) A game theoretic analysis of the inter-American convention against corruption. Available at: https://heinonline.org/HOL/LandingPage?handle=hein.journals/rjnglbs16&div=9&id=&page=. Consulted on 11 Nov 2025

Pinto NR (2020) A importância do monitoramento constante das operações e do dever de colaboração na prevenção à lavagem de dinheiro no mercado de capitais. In: Souza LA (coord) Compliance no Direito Penal. Revista dos Tribunais, São Paulo

Ragués i Vallès R (2006) ¿Héroes o traidores? La protección de los informantes internos (whistleblowers) como estrategia político-criminal. InDret, pp 1–19

Ragués i Vallès R (2013) Whistleblowing: una aproximación desde el derecho penal. Editora Marcial Pons, Madrid

Reilly PR (2014) Ralph Lauren, transnational bribery and voluntary disclosure under the foreign corrupt practices act: when is it strategically wise (or not) to self-report FCPA violations to the SEC? Harvard Business Law Review

Rodríguez VG, Saad-Diniz E, Marin GC (2020) Programas de whistleblowing e os problemas da delação premiada. In: Souza LA (coord) Compliance no Direito Penal. Revista dos Tribunais, São Paulo

Saad-Diniz E (2013a) Nova Lei de Lavagem de Dinheiro no Brasil: compreendendo os programas de 'criminal compliance.' Revista Digital Do IAB 18:99–107

Saad-Diniz E (2013b) O modelo brasileiro de prevenção à lavagem de dinheiro: as repercussões da Ação Penal 470. Boletim IBCCRIM, São Paulo, 21(242):9–10, Jan

Saad-Diniz E, Silveira RDMJ (2015) Compliance, Direito Penal e Lei Anticorrupção. Saraiva, São Paulo

Scaff FF, Silveira RDMJ (2014) Lei Anticorrupção é substancialmente de caráter penal. Consultor Juridico, 5 Feb

Sheperd KL (2012) Business: the gatekeeper initiative and the risk-based approach to client due diligence. The Review of Banking and Financial Services

Silva Sánchez JM (2009) Tiempos del derecho penal. BdeF, Madrid

Silveira RDMJ (2018) Bitcoin e suas fronteiras penais: em busca do marco penal das criptomoedas. D'Plácido, Belo Horizonte

Silveira RDMJ (2020) Direito Penal da era compliance, a realidade penal econômico-empresarial brasileira e a variação de seus momentos. In: Souza LA (coord) Compliance no Direito Penal. Revista dos Tribunais, São Paulo

Silveira RDMJ, Saad-Diniz E (2013) Criminal compliance: os limites da cooperação normativa quanto à lavagem de dinheiro. Revista peruana de ciencias penales, Lima, n.25

Sun M (2025) Despite enforcement pause, ignoring antibribery law still raises risks for companies. Wall Street Journal, 11 Mar

Tarun RW (2011) A Baker's Dozen: practical FCPA advice for multinational executives, General Counsel and Audit Committees

Verhage A (2008) Between the hammer and the anvil? The anti-money laundering-complex and its interactions with the compliance industry. Crime Law Soc. Change, Nov.

Chapter 3
Implementation of a *Compliance* Programme

In discussing the structure and fundamentals of *compliance* programmes, Adán Nieto Martín explains that there are *common elements*, which are necessary for the implementation of an effective programme and *quality criteria* that should be observed to prevent controls from being ineffective or, as he asserts, *façade programmes.* The company must initially decide whether to implement a model simply focused on monitoring its employees and collaborators or a model affirming ethical values and linked to the notion of corporate social responsibility and business ethics.[1]

One of the author's concerns is that *compliance* programmes are used solely as defence mechanisms in the event of potential legal proceedings, without a real concern for prevention and supervision duties. To avoid this path, among the *common elements* to all programmes, one should consider:

(i) risk analysis (closely related to the type of market in which the company operates);

(ii) the implementation of codes of ethics, through which behavioural guidelines will be outlined;

(iii) internal controls and *due diligence* with suppliers and external collaborators;

(iv) constant training and communication, so that policies do not get lost in corporate *intranets* and duties and obligations are known to all;

(v) mechanisms for detecting irregularities and the provision of sanctions, as well as positive incentives;

(vi) pre-determined response protocols, so that the company knows how to handle negative news and potential damage repair, if necessary;

(vii) institutionalisation of the programme when those responsible for supervision and coordination of areas related to *compliance* will be appointed;

(viii) periodic evaluation of the measures implemented and, finally,

(ix) documentation of the entire system put into practice.[2]

As for *quality criteria*, the following are highlighted:

---

[1] Nieto Martín (2019a, b, p. 103).

[2] Nieto Martín (2019d, pp. 149–152).

L. A. d. Souza and N. R. Pinto, *Criminal Compliance – Concepts and Implementation*,
https://doi.org/10.1007/978-3-032-15011-0_3

(i) the necessary involvement of senior executives, through their daily behaviour, in the dissemination of good practices and expected behaviours;

(ii) the important participation of all *stakeholders* linked to the company's activity;

(iii) the coherence between the formal system and organisational culture;

(iv) the training and ability of those who are assigned to implement the programme, as well as their:

(v) indispensable independence and the necessary existence of sufficient human and material resources.[3]

All these points are of utmost importance and culminate in a final characteristic which is organisational culture, which can be defined as "*the values, customs and traditions*" of a particular company that will guide and influence its mode of operation, internally and externally.[4]

3.1 Position of *Compliance* Within Corporate Structures

The multidisciplinary nature of *compliance* and the division of tasks in vertical and horizontal corporate structures present us with an interesting discussion related to organisational structure: after all, where should compliance be? The alignment with the legal department seems natural when considered from the perspective of the necessary knowledge of the regulatory frameworks of the economic sector to which the company belongs.

However, maintaining *compliance* integrated with the company's legal department could cause the two activities to conflict: the development of training, policies, and internal standards could interfere, for example, with meeting legal deadlines, which would result in one of the areas being relegated to the background. Others may argue that proximity to the areas of internal controls, or even with the monitoring and supervision techniques performed by audits, has the power to influence the shift of *compliance* towards this side.

Furthermore, as we previously mentioned, the independence of *compliance* policies is one of the main characteristics to be ensured in an effective programme. Thus, the correct model will be the one that guarantees, within the corporate structure, autonomy and access to the information produced by the various areas that make up the organisation.

To gain access to all sectors, the *compliance* cannot be linked to any. Moreover, considering the strategic role of the legal department, such a connection could, in some way, harm the dependence that must be maintained by the *compliance* area.

The *compliance* area should be thought of as separate from the corporate hierarchical structure and should report its activities only to the administrative collegial bodies. It is worth noting that *compliance* is not, and cannot be treated as, an executive body which would be responsible for decision-making.

[3] Nieto Martín (2019, pp. 153–154).

[4] Steinberg (2011, p. 5).

Its function involves, from monitoring and risk analysis, indicating to the effectively competent subjects the result of its checks, leaving it to them to take measures they deem necessary. That being said, having collaborators from various areas of the company seems to be a strategically correct approach.

On the subject, Silveira states that "*by detecting potential problems, and making the ideal communication of them, its filter proves adequate, passing the responsibility to the delegating body, which will ultimately be responsible for implementing the final policies of the legal entity*".[5] This approach has the potential to maintain corporate integrity and dynamics.

One of the most sensitive points in Economic Criminal Law is to determine what the *responsibility* of each of the subjects who are part of the corporate structure is. On rare occasions, the decision-making centre will be close to the practice of irregularity, which will complicate the task of the prosecution bodies when attributing responsibilities or favouring objective liability.

The case of Embraer, analysed *infra*, is a good example of the complexity of corporate decision-making structures, involving several meetings, endless chains of *emails* that, often, involve the participation of various areas of the company. As Estellita states, "*the larger the company structure* [...] *the more complex the process from decision-making to its execution will be, usually involving various vertical and horizontal layers*".[6]

In this context, it is necessary to determine what are the possible actions that can be put into practice by the *compliance* department. Focused on preventive conception, its tasks include the implementation of effective internal controls that allow the identification of possible irregularities, within the sensitive fields to business activity.[7] From this point, it is not up to the *compliance* area to make decisions that may prevent improper outcomes, but to communicate the risks to those who hold the effective capacity within the organisational structure.

Considering this limitation of action, we highlight that the *compliance* department, if properly structured, represents an advisory area of corporate administration, not having veto power over decisions made in the business sphere.[8]

Considering this context of possible attributions of criminal responsibilities, it will be fundamental to define transparently and document the attributions of each area and collaborator, so that there is no creation of wrong expectations about the role played by each one. It is not acceptable, especially in the criminal sphere, the attribution of automatic responsibilities without considering the factual aspects of the function performed within the organisational structure.

---

5 Silveira and Saa-Diniz (2015, p. 145).

6 Estellita (2015).

7 Costa and Araújo (2014, p. 222).

8 Costa and Araújo (2014, p. 223).

This is, in fact, the understanding of the SEC, the US federal agency regulating financial markets, which published guidance prohibiting the attribution of responsibility to the subject simply because they hold a position in the area of *compliance*.[9] This understanding brings security to those who work in the sector.

It is noteworthy that the subtlety of the role of *compliance* lies in the fact that, while it is not a department responsible for hiring or firing employees, it will have the function of influencing everyone to observe the rules related to the corporation's operations. It will be responsible for ensuring the observance of the rules and procedures followed within the company, but not for decision-making.

More than that, it will be an internal *gatekeeper* focused on the functions required by the State for monitoring and investigation, without effectively exercising control over people. However, there is no normative provision about the role to be played by the person responsible for *compliance;* it is only known that they will need to keep the company's activity within the allowed risks.

This does not mean that it is the agent's role to prevent possible irregularities, but it will be the duty of the *compliance* department to report to the responsible bodies. Their vision, therefore, will be generalist and dynamic, focusing on the supervision of controls and not people, and with the aim of reporting any failures to the administrators and managers of the area where the problem was identified.

The independence of the *compliance* area, especially with relation to the so-called *power centres,*[10] constitutes one of the most important pillars of its implementation, which is why its autonomy should reflect in the reporting duty to be made, only, to the Board of Directors. For example, in an internal investigation about the conduct of a statutory director of a public company, the possible hierarchy in the reports could compromise the work and the conduct of activities. The fact that *compliance* only presents reports to the Board will, then, be fundamental in proving its performance.

This is an area that will work closely and coordinately with all other sectors of the company, which is why communication and the flow of constant information should be a priority. The goal of risk detection can only be met in this way.

It should be emphasised, in this sense, the relevance of access to information being ensured, as widely publicised in anti-money laundering regulations. A company that does not have effective transparency policies cannot claim to have implemented a well-established *compliance*, even if formally it has all the necessary characteristics.

It is important to note that the *compliance* area should be available to all company employees, be easily accessible, and widely publicised. For this, the training carried out will be decisive in informing the entire company about the existence of this area, its duties, and responsibilities.

If, at first, the members of the *compliance* area are not considered as effective delegates of the business owners, the situation changes if, in practice, they are responsible for making executive decisions. From the moment they start to have control of the results that are achieved, one can consider duties of guarantee, of controlling the production of risks beyond those allowed.

---

[9] Martin (2015, pp. 175) and following.

[10] Nieto Martín (2012, p. 125).

The opposite is also true, that is, the business owner cannot think that they will no longer have responsibilities simply because they have symbolically implemented internal controls. The *compliance* does not constitute, by itself, a shield of responsibilities.

3.2 Engagement of Senior Management

In studying the causes of irregular behaviours within corporations, Sutherland pointed out that state norms and internal statutes would have little importance, as control instruments, if they did not have the support of corporate management.[11] In this vein, it is noted that a large part of the success of a *compliance* programme will be related to the way in which management and senior management will propagate the culture and expected behaviours. Their commitment should reflect in the actions and decisions taken in the daily activities of the company, in order to show that there is a culture of non-tolerance to violations of internal rules and regulations.

For Nieto Martín, the participation of senior management can be seen as a beneficial factor for not-so-well-implemented programmes, while their non-integration would harm the most robust and sophisticated internal controls.[12] This understanding can be easily exemplified with the centralising CEOs of Enron and WorldCom companies who, constantly, claimed that *compliance* policies were not relevant or necessary.

In addition to them, Boards of Directors that are not very engaged can be quite harmful, in terms of corporate governance, if they do not demand information or, in possession of these, fail to request measures aimed at controlling or eliminating the identified risks.

In the previous section, it was considered that simply occupying a position within the organisational structure is not sufficient to assign responsibilities, but rather that each member of the executive bodies must perform their tasks in a way that ensures corporate activities are kept within the permitted risks. The existence of adequate information flows and the ability to operate within the business structure play a significant role in this discussion.

It is even recommended that all decisions and assemblies held are properly recorded through minutes, especially if there are dissenting votes or expressions.

Even though they are not directly responsible for the implementation of the *compliance* metrics put into practice, the Board of Directors, for example, should analyse and supervise, through the reports made by the *compliance* area, whether the controls are suitable for the company's reality.[13]

We have studied in the anti-money laundering and anti-corruption regulations that the participation and support of senior management are essential for internal controls

[11] Sutherland (2015, p. 375).

[12] Nieto Martín (2019, pp. 74–75).

[13] Steinberg (2012, p. 6).

not to be merely symbolic and formal. Guidelines published by international and Brazilian bodies highlight the importance of leaders' commitment to *compliance* programmes.

The *Anti-Corruption Ethics and Compliance Handbook for Business,* published by the OECD in 2013, states that effective internal controls depend on the visible support and engagement of senior management (*"tone from the top").* Among the functions assigned to the most relevant hierarchical members are:

> (i) ensuring that all employees and collaborators, internal and external, as well as business partners are aware of the values and standards governing the corporation;
>
> (ii) given the complexity of monitoring all the company's daily activities, they should establish capable individuals responsible for developing and monitoring the implemented policies;
>
> (iii) providing the *compliance* areas with necessary resources so they can carry out their activities and
>
> (iv) putting their support into practice through public interactions with the collaborators.[14]

The CGU, in 2015, published Guidelines for private companies related to the implementation of integrity programmes, through which it defined the commitment of senior management as *"the foundation for creating an organisational culture in which employees and third parties truly value ethical conduct"*.[15] According to the Guidelines, the participation of the highest members of the hierarchy in harmful acts determines the *"absence of institutional commitment"* to internal controls.

The engagement of senior management can be proven, if necessary, through the actions carried out in the company's daily life, such as, for example, the institutional and financial support given to the *compliance* area. The existence of a team dedicated to the implementation of internal controls is not enough if the executive does not demonstrate its importance through internal communications, participation in training, and engagement proposals, through which the importance of training and the values shared by the company would be explained.

The guidelines tend to focus on senior management, but we believe that the importance of intermediate management levels should also be considered, as long as they are responsible for teams and other collaborators, for example. This person tends to be the first point of doubt for those who are unsure about their conduct or what would be the most appropriate decision for a given situation.

In this context, the engagement of managers in the implementation of good practices will be decisive in ensuring the expected behaviour. More than being able to direct behaviour, part of the managerial role will involve monitoring their team, not in a policing aspect, but with the aim of maintaining proximity, for cases where there may be, for example, confusion between doing the right thing and achieving the established goals.

An ethical organisational culture focused on good corporate practices is the main point of *compliance* programmes and will be built in the daily activities of the

[14] OECD: *Anti-Corruption Ethics and Compliance Handbook for Business*, 2013.

[15] General Comptroller of the Union. *Integrity Programme: Guidelines for Private Companies*, 2015.

business, through the assimilation of the values that the corporation understands as aligned with its governance structure. Thus, administrators, as focal points of the company, should encourage all *stakeholders* to participate in the building of these ethical values and aimed at the development of the company.

3.3 Internal Codes of Ethics

One of the most delicate points in the implementation of internal *compliance* programmes is the development of the concept of what will be determined as ethical behaviour or even what is the expected conduct of collaborators, at all levels of the organisation. Here, there will be a great influence of what is sought to establish as "*a corporate culture, as well as the values that are sought to be propagated, adapting this discourse for internal and external implementation.*"

The establishment of an ethical culture with business entities considered as good corporate citizens holds this aspect as fundamental.

Considering that it is a real corporate challenge, defining the culture and ethical standards that will guide the daily life of employees will involve more than (the already complicated mission of) finding a trivial concept of what is ethical, especially in the complex environment of economic activities. The difficulty related to identifying a common denominator should be considered, with an even greater challenge for large transnational companies, which will need to think about policies applicable in different legal systems and realities.

The establishment of good corporate governance concerned with the prevention of agency costs, with the harmony of the *stakeholders* and seeking to go beyond the so-called *shareholder value*, will require an internal commitment especially from senior management. As seen in the previous item, the concern of those who hold the highest positions in highlighting the importance of good practices will be decisive in the development of an ethical environment.

Lynn Paine differentiates the measures put into practice in the implementation of *compliance* programmes from those aimed at developing what she calls *organisational integrity*. In her view, the ethical standard should be determined according to the values defended by the corporation, being something to be applied in its daily life naturally and not through the imposition of sanctions, which, on the contrary, would be counterproductive.[16]

Richard Steinberg, on the other hand, characterises culture as the most prominent point in the implementation of a *compliance* programme.[17] In our opinion, it is necessary to follow both authors, considering that formal prevention procedures will not be effectively applied if there is not the backing of an organisational culture oriented towards correct action.

---

[16] Paine (1994). Available at: https://hbr.org/1994/03/managing-for-organizational-integrity. Accessed on 11 November 2025.

[17] Steinberg (2012, p. 6).

In this context, Internal or Ethical Codes can be characterised as *soft law* norms that, with the intention of promoting or boosting business ethics,[18] will establish mandatory rules for employees and disciplinary sanctions for their respective violations.[19] Although it is emphasised that the sanctioning character should not guide the Internal Codes, research indicates that they tend to be developed much more as procedural defence mechanisms of the company than as instruments committed to the development of corporate social responsibility.[20] At this point, it seems important to us to highlight brief explanations about the importance and, more than that, the existing connection between internal controls and corporate governance.

At first, we highlight that companies, from a corporate social responsibility (*corporate social responsibility*) perspective, will have rights and duties that must be observed internally and externally, taking into account all *stakeholders* who, in some way, may be impacted by the activities developed.

Corporate governance policies are related to internal decision-making processes, especially when considering the reality that companies are no longer solely controlled by their owners, but by administrators selected because of their specialisation. It is up to corporate governance, therefore, to develop values and models of action that should be observed by business management.

For this, it is necessary to ensure compliance with information duties, transparency, and accessibility to those responsible, and, in this context, harmonise the interests of all *stakeholders* (it is important to highlight the overcoming of management independence models focused solely on the returns generated to *stockholders*, as defended by Friedman in the 70s of the twentieth century[21]).

As social, economic, and political actors, companies need, legitimately, to include within their concerns and objectives the relationship maintained with their surroundings (here understood as, for example, the environment, consumers, local communities).[22]

Internal Codes are the documents that should establish the internal values of the company, determine the expected behaviors and set the tone of corporate governance, as Nieto Martín affirms. For the author, ethical codes represent the *cornerstone* of the *compliance* system, which is why they have a binding character and need to be aligned with the company's culture.[23]

From the moment they guide behavioural expectations and condition how employees need to act in their daily activities, this perspective understands that documents need to acquire legitimacy, which could be achieved through the participation of all stakeholders in their formulation.[24] As a policy that will guide and bind

18 Nieto Martín (2013, p. 24).

19 Rodrigues (2018, p. 20).

20 Stevens (1994, pp. 66–67).

21 Friedman (1970).

22 Nieto Martín (2019, p. 45).

23 Nieto Martín (2019, pp. 163–165).

24 Nieto Martín (2019, pp. 170) and following.

all company representatives,[25] having representatives from all areas proves to be of great importance in its preparation.

As there needs to be coherence between published policies and the behaviour of representatives, business ethics will be developed in two main aspects: the *normative ethics*, developed, theoretically, to guide the company's behaviour, and the *applied ethics*, as the name suggests, in the dilemmas faced in everyday life.[26] It should be noted that the ethical standard sought will not be achieved through formal documents or even through disciplinary sanctions applied.

The sanctions provided for by internal codes can be identified as intersecting with the principle of *ultima ratio*, which underpins, or should underpin, the application of criminal laws. Just like the punishments defined by the state, the company will determine sanctions applicable to violations of its internal rules after proportionality examinations.

It should be noted that the sanctions provided for should, just like in criminal law, have a character of prevention, education, and reintegration of offenders. Therefore, dismissals, for example, should only be applied as a last resort, considering the high impact it can have on the employee's life and the low effectiveness of practices if a failing and inadequate culture environment is observed.

However, the focus of internal Codes of Conduct should not be the establishment of *enforcement* measures, but to clearly portray the values internalised in the corporation and the expected behaviour of all employees, regardless of their position. Furthermore, although the focus on the sanctions provided for in case of violation of the rules has been noticed, few Codes provide for internal sanctioning procedures, highlighting the difficulty of communicating to employees their rights and duties.[27]

Various individual situations can influence the development of undesirable cultures within the business scope. Exaggerated goals, focus on results, competitive climate, coupled with social pressures for success, can lead an employee astray.

These wrong incentives can distort the results sought by internal norms. Hui Chen and Eugene Soltes highlight that, in a survey conducted with 3,000 executives, 42% responded that they could justify unethical behaviours that had occurred to achieve financial objectives.[28] Many cases of behavioural deviations use the pursuit of more advantageous results as a justification for improper conduct.

For everyone to feel like part of a larger project and for there to be an understanding of the objectives sought, the importance of *stakeholder democracy*, the participation of everyone in the development of the rules,[29] is discussed. More than gathering all stakeholders in a room to discuss each point, which would be unfeasible in more complex business structures, what is considered are general participations to raise the most relevant aspects and the existence of openings for questions and doubts.

---

[25] Barbosa and Olivé (2019, p. 196).

[26] Nieto Martín (2019, p. 48).

[27] Stevens (1994, pp. 66–67).

[28] Chen and Solter (2020). Available at: https://hbr.org/2018/03/why-compliance-programs-fail. Accessed on 11 November 2025.

[29] Nieto Martín (2013, p. 35).

In this way, internal codes should be drawn up after the completion of risk assessments made by the *compliance* area, since its action will not be able to cover all the daily situations of the company, only those that are most important and require more attention. In addition to determining the corporation's values, the codes of ethics establish expected behaviour rules and define potential responsibilities that may be applied in case of non-compliance with existing rules.[30]

Considering its widespread application, and also because internal codes tend to expand the functions provided for in employment contracts, it is required that they are clear and easily accessible. Although directed at all employees, the Code of Conduct may establish additional duties for managers regarding the promotion of the rules provided by the company and the reporting of irregularities of which they are aware.

Examples of behaviour expected by a company include correct action within the corporation, collaborating with the development of colleagues up to the prohibition of prejudiced behaviours in the work environment. Possible conflicts of interest that may in some way influence internal decisions should be reported to the responsible internal bodies, such as designated Ethics Committees, for evaluation of the received communications.

Examples of points of attention regarding conduct include the political expression of employees, opinions expressed in seminars and lectures, especially if related to the activities carried out by the company. It is worth highlighting the emphasise given to reputational values when implementing *compliance* programmes and internal controls, particularly with the development and expansion of the use of social media.

How to handle and take care of internal information, the mandatory confidentiality required by law (such as in the case of significant facts not published to the market), up to the disposal of documents, considering protection standards, can be addressed by internal codes. Finally, it is important that the document provides important internal contacts, such as phone numbers and *emails* that can be accessed by those who have relevant information and, no less important, by those who have any doubts about how to proceed in specific situations.

In practice, the codes already specify what sanctions may be applied in case of violation of the guidelines discussed. After internal investigations, applicable penalties may include formal warnings, suspensions, or even termination or ending of the contractual relationship between employee and employer.

An interesting example of this is the case of the Siemens company in Germany. After the scandal involving the internalisation of bribe payments as standard accounting (*Untreue*), the company was required to include a specific provision in its Code of Conduct prohibiting the practice.[31]

Codes of Conduct usually include internal rules related to the receipt of gifts and hospitality, for example. Knowing when to accept participation in events promoted by suppliers, identifying when the benefits are related to the position held within

---

30 Nieto Martín (2019, p. 171).

31 Nieto Martín (2019, p. 78).

the company, and cases in which invitations to parties and dinners may even require specific authorisations and approvals.

Codes of Conduct should also make it clear that they bind all company employees, from its highest administrators to interns. All people who provide services, even if temporary or outsourced, should also pay attention to the premises and values determined by the corporation (it is common for there to be specific codes for suppliers and outsourced workers).

It should be noted, however, that the Code does not provide solutions and answers for every situation faced by its representatives, but its objective is to provide guidelines and rules of behaviour and conduct to be adopted on a daily basis. This is what characterises risk management.

3.4 Training: How to Apply and How to Measure the Efficiency of the Programme

Nieto Martin divides the implementation of *compliance* programmes into two models: (i) those focused on the code of ethics, which seek to develop a climate of respect for norms, and (ii) others based on surveillance and control measures.[32] The choice made in this work, when explaining the essential points of internal compliance programmes, was the first; after all, it is not agreed with the theory that internal controls should be an expansion of repressive Criminal Law, but that they should act preventively and for the development of an ethical business perspective.

That said, a well-structured and properly implemented *compliance* programme is of no use if the company's employees are not aware of the rules provided, what behaviours are expected and also those that are undesirable. In this sense, a fundamental step to determine the effectiveness of the programmes is the regular training that should be applied to the entire corporation, from newly hired interns to the presidency and Board of Directors.

More than making everyone aware of the internal rules, the trainings will be decisive in identifying areas for improvement and in which areas the employees have been having more doubts and therefore require more attention.

With the trainings, the company's real commitment to the dissemination of its internal policies and the development of an appropriate organisational culture can be perceived. It is argued that the trainings can be presented to *enforcement* bodies as strong evidence that employees, at least, should be aware of the expected and prohibited behaviours, simply by delivering documents that prove the application of *workshops,* lectures, and the well-known *PowerPoints* available on internal networks. The challenge, however, is not so much related to the application of trainings, but to proving their effectiveness.

A paradigmatic example can be given with the hypothesis in which, on a Monday, an *email* informs the employee about the need to carry out a new training on, e.g.,

[32] Nieto Martín (2013, p. 33).

money laundering in a financial institution. The employee, with several accumulated demands, is then quickly reminded by his manager about the alleged importance of all trainings being duly completed by the end of the week. Depending on the company, the demand may even be accompanied by a financial impact on variable remuneration in the event of a delay in completing the aforementioned course. However, the importance of the topic addressed is not discussed, let alone how that content will influence the activities performed by the employee.

On Friday, the aforementioned employee decides to do the training quickly, between one task, *truly important*, and another. At the end of the day, their manager receives the *email* informing that all the training has been successfully completed by the team. Commonly, no matter the subject, whether it's information security, fraud prevention or practices related to corruption, the plot is the same.

The small story told will repeat itself in larger or smaller companies if the important role of training is not highlighted and explained to all employees. More than just another task to be squeezed into busy schedules, training should be applied with the aim of integrating the corporate member into the values and cultures proposed and planned by the company. If we think that one of the most used indicators by companies is the number of trainings carried out, our busy employee will only highlight the symbolic aspect of the internal controls implemented.

From the moment the *compliance* programme is designed with the sole aim of complying with what is formally expected by the standard, without thinking about how its structures should reflect the reality of the company, even if hundreds of thousands of reais are spent, little effectiveness will be shown in practical terms. As Chen and Soltes argue, implementing programmes with the sole aim of fitting within what is expected by the standard tends to reduce the chances of positively influencing employee behaviour.[33]

As mentioned in the caricatured story, often the training will be seen as a *waste of time*, which is why the language needs to be attractive and suitable for the target audience. The employee needs to understand the purpose of that activity and how they can apply those teachings in their daily activities.

Therefore, it is recommended that theoretical explanations be accompanied by practical examples and guidance on how to solve problems that may be faced on a daily basis. Concrete examples tend to bring the training closer to the activities performed by the employees, moving away from the *slides* that may not bring the necessary attention and engagement.

Just like all aspects of *compliance* programmes, training needs to be dynamic and constantly updated. Dynamism also includes offering specific training for areas with distinct risk assignments.

For example, departments that have the activity of signing contracts with public bodies need to have a greater understanding of anti-corruption rules and international accounting registration requirements, in the case of publicly traded companies. Different realities demand different knowledge. Standardized training for the

[33] Chen and Soltes (2018).

entire corporation indicates formal *compliance* programs and little effectiveness for the purpose they propose.

Just as tasks vary between departments, the language should be designed to reach all employees, regardless of existing prior knowledge. Excessive technical terms can be explained through more palatable presentations, ensuring the translation of information and adapting internal requirements to standards and peculiarities, in the case of multinational companies operating in more than one country.

Another important point to mention is the format of the training presentation: *online* or face-to-face? While the former can be more dynamic and reach a larger number of employees, the latter allows for greater interaction and more effective participation, as there will be full attention and the possibility of clearing up any doubts that may arise. Thus, the company needs to evaluate, within its costs and availability, the best methodology to be applied, and may even offer different training according to its needs.

A highlight when dealing with corporate training is the understanding, by the employees, of the objectives behind those rules and how they influence their daily lives. Here, the use of technological tools that allow formal training to be carried out throughout the business chain becomes important, not forgetting the evaluation of what has been learnt.

If possible, it is relevant to ask questions before the actual training, to verify what has been understood and the information whose assimilation will require more attention from the receiver and, perhaps, a better strategy from the sharer. *Feedback* on the format can identify whether the explanations were clear or if it is necessary to address a certain subject in a more didactic way.

In addition to formal training, companies can think of other ways to communicate their internal policies and expected behaviours to their employees. *Emails* and *newsletters* with main points and practical examples can be sent to different internal areas; posters spread in common areas of the company allow effective communication that will be easily assimilated; the promotion of events and lectures that deal with the company's activity are also good examples of ways to approach the *compliance of the employees.*

It is emphasised that all training conducted should be properly recorded. In the case of Morgan Stanley, e.g., as analyzed below, the proof that director Garth Peterson had access to the expected behaviour and internal rules of the institution, on several occasions, was decisive for the dosimetry of the sanction. Conversely, e.g., in the case of Madero, the CGU understood that, although there were threats from public employees demanding undue advantages, the *compliance* programme failed to establish the expected conduct of its employees. Provisions such as the immediate rejection of any illicit request and subsequent internal reporting could have been anticipated.

The trainings then highlight the importance of technology in propagating the correct values and attitudes. With them, those responsible for the policies will have access to consolidated data, accurate information and updated reports that will facilitate the identification of points of attention and necessary improvements.[34] More

---

[34] Steinberg (2011, pp. 34–35).

than tools to *tick the box*, the trainings will be great allies in the development of the correct organisational culture that is sought to be promoted with the *compliance* programmes.

3.5 Internal Whistleblowing Channels

Within the logic of public–private collaboration, whistleblowing channels, or *hotlines*, will occupy a prominent place in companies as effective mechanisms for obtaining information that would hardly be discovered otherwise. The flow of information within a company is one of the most sensitive aspects when considering the implementation of internal controls and, therefore, it is necessary to ensure that the strategy used by the company to deal with what is received will be appropriate.

As Steinberg asserts, there are three words that summarise the importance of information channels: *monitoring*, *testing*, and *supervision*.[35] It was previously verified that *compliance* programmes cannot be static.

From monitoring the areas of attention in the company, the programmes should reflect all the modifications that are necessary to meet regulatory requirements, thinking from the macro aspect to internal points of attention, such as, for example, an area in which a larger number of alerts from employees are reported or even the occurrence of more serious communications.

Along with codes of conduct, *hotlines* are highlighted by Wellner as one of the basic elements of a *compliance* programme.[36] Characterized as internal or external *whistleblowers*, the holders of information play a relevant role in the policy of prevention of economic crime.

Initially, it should be categorised that a *whistleblower*, in this explanation, will be the one who reports an illicit act, of which they became aware, that occurred within the corporate structure to which they are linked.[37]

An *internal* informant will be considered to be the one who reports the irregularity to the channels provided by the corporation itself, or *external*, if they take the information directly to public authorities or media.

It is emphasised that the *whistleblower* constitutes a figure different from the informer, which will be studied later. This is a subject who, in some way, participated in the illicit conduct and, for the purpose of procedural advantage, chooses to inform the authorities of the details of what they know, while the former would inform the communication channels of an irregularity to which they had access, without necessarily having any participation.

An example of an internal *whistleblower* can be cited as the aforementioned case of WorldCom, whose accounting frauds were discovered by the internal audit team, especially from the analysis of auditor Cynthia Cooper, when suspecting records of

[35] Steinberg (2012, p. 8).

[36] Wellner (2005, p. 501).

[37] García-Moreno (2020, p. 27).

financial transactions that, in reality, were false operational costs inserted to inflate the company's profits.[38] As an example of an external *whistleblower*, in turn, there is Hervé Falciani, a former employee of HSBC in Switzerland, who leaked data from thousands of undeclared accounts and, supposedly, involved in tax evasion.[39]

An interesting aspect of the case is that Falciani initially struggled to find parties interested in publishing the information he had.

The concept of the *whistleblower* is not exactly a recent phenomenon and has been regulated, particularly in the USA, for some time.[40] Initially, the regulations were focused on individual rights, but over time, *whistleblowers* have become increasingly important in criminal policy related to information control.[41]

In the American legal system, where the involvement of informants is not necessarily disinterested,[42] the discussion is solidly regulated by laws such as the *False Claims Act*, *FCPA*, *SOX*, and *Dodd-Frank*. These laws highlight the importance of *whistleblowers* and intensify the prohibition of retaliation against those who bring information to the competent authorities, as well as establishing a reward of up to 30% of what is obtained from the prosecution of offenders. This point becomes more delicate especially because it involves remunerations that can reach considerable amounts, which would make the informant seek external reporting channels as a first option,[43] weakening the efforts put into practice by internal *compliance*.

In other countries, however, the discussion is more delicate, with concerns that instead of promoting compliance with norms, internal channels may develop a climate of constant surveillance and denunciation.[44] To avoid this, companies should establish clear policies on what information should be reported, how, and what internal procedures will be implemented to investigate what is received. This point will be better analysed in the next section, related to the development of internal codes.

Generally, employees tend to report an irregularity identified in their work routine to an internal body that they believe will be able to act to stop the practice or prevent new occurrences.[45] This reception of information and subsequent reporting to responsible areas can be seen as one of the functions of the *compliance* department.[46]

The process of seeking reporting channels involves four elements[47]:

---

[38] Pinto (2017, p. 29).

[39] Barbosa and Olivé (2019, p. 204).

[40] According to the historical evolution made by Artur de Brito Gueiros Souza, the first protection for informants, in the USA, would date back to 30th July 1778 and would be related to a complaint made by a captain about the excesses committed by a commander during the American Revolution. Souza (2020, p. 35).

[41] Rodríguez et al. (2020, p. 91).

[42] Barbosa and Olivé (2019, p. 200).

[43] Steinberg (2011, p. 48).

[44] Ragués I Vallès (2013, p. 36).

[45] García-Moreno (2020, p. 61).

[46] Barbosa and Olivé (2019, p. 193).

[47] Near and Miceli (1985, p. 2) and following.

(i) the *whistleblower* (the individual who, at some point, had a connection with the organisation and who did not have the capacity to change the identified irregularity);

(ii) the reported act (information disclosed with the intention of preventing harm to third parties or the public interest);

(iii) the party receiving the information (whether from an internal or external *whistleblower*) and, finally,

(iv) the involved organisation.

While countries like France stipulate that the *whistleblower's* action should be disinterested, the UK requires that there be public interest involved, while others, like the USA, as mentioned earlier, encourage the disclosure of information, especially to public authorities, and offer financial rewards (incentives) for this, as verified in the Dodd-Frank Act.[48]

Precisely because of the complexity of the instrument, which will not always be accessed with the aim of stopping an irregularity, and the serious personal and employment effects that can be generated for those involved, it is necessary to consider a point of great relevance. The involvement of the company as a victim or beneficiary will also be significant for the following discussion.

Much is said about the importance of *hotlines* being anonymous, either for fear of retaliation, to facilitate or even stimulate more employees to report information they are aware of. Therefore, there is a difference to be considered between reports being anonymous or confidential.

The person being investigated must be informed about the opening of the investigations internally. Confidentiality ensures that only those responsible for the investigation have access to the information, often confidential.[49] Thus, the head of a particular department will not (or at least should not) have access to the source of the complaint, thereby avoiding potential persecutions and reprisals within the company.

It should be kept in mind that reporting an irregularity—which may have been committed by a colleague—will be a very difficult decision for the *whistleblower*, especially considering the negative consequences they may face. In addition to the possible proximity to the person who committed the irregularity, there are the duties of loyalty and good faith contracted between the informant and the company.[50]

In this context, personal issues such as the position held, career goals, length of service, self-esteem, chance of getting a similar job, and the support of colleagues and family will be decisive for the decision to proceed with the action of reporting.[51]

---

[48] García-Moreno (2020, p. 71) and following.

[49] Ragués I Vallès (2013, p. 65) and following.

[50] Ragués I Vallès (2006, p. 12).

[51] Near and Miceli (s, p. 5) and following.

According to a document published by the G20, which highlights twelve principles aimed at protecting *whistleblowers,* the risk of corruption practices increases in environments where the reporting of information is not encouraged and protected.[52]

Among the principles considered are:

(i) the importance of legal systems having protection rules for those who report irregularities and that this practice is also encouraged for companies;
(ii) the channels for receiving complaints should be visible and widely disseminated, and companies should have procedures for handling the information received;
(iii) ensure the confidentiality of all parties involved;
(iv) establish rules that inform which behaviours will be considered retaliations and which instruments can be sought by *whistleblowers* who need assistance;
(v) ensure that there will be no liability for those who seek the complaint channels, except for cases where the prior knowledge of the falsity of the information is proven, when there may even be compensations for people who have been involved and harmed by the false reports.

As mentioned, the figure of the one who brings to light an infraction of a colleague or even a superior will not always be seen as a courageous act, and may trigger practices such as persecution in the workplace, harassment, or even dismissal. The perspective of disloyalty can also arise depending on the type of organisational culture in practice.

For this reason, regulations must remain attentive to the incentives and protections that will be offered so that people report irregularities they are aware of, and it is up to companies to convey the importance of these channels for building a well-structured company internally.

Other criticisms of the *whistleblower* institution are related to the role that begins to be required of employees, of a possible surveillance of their colleagues, which could impact the organisational climate, and the chance of a person being exposed and stigmatised without the existence of a formal accusation.[53]

The company must, therefore, be cautious when implementing complaint channels with clear and precise information about their operation, seeking to avoid subjective criteria, such as good faith, and moral aspects as points that may influence the employee's decision to communicate what they know. The search for complaint channels will show that employees understand the need to report any failures, showing that the ethical and prevention culture is working, regardless of financial incentives or regulatory obligations.

The absence of search may be an indication that there is nothing to worry about, and that, in fact, irregularities are not committed within the company, or that there is a lack of trust on the part of employees that the reported information will be effectively treated, or that there will be no eventual retaliation.

---

[52] Information available at: https://www.unodc.org/documents/corruption/G20-Anti-Corruption-Resources/Thematic-Areas/Public-Sector-Integrity-and-Transparency/G20_High-Level_Principles_for_the_Effective_Protection_of_Whistleblowers_2019.pdf. Accessed on 11 November 2025.

[53] Souza (2020, p. 40).

In its commitment to preventing irregularities, the company should use the complaint channel as a source of information about what deserves more attention and what poses greater risks in its operation. Thus, the management of the channel will be determinant for the success of the *compliance* programme.

Considering that often the information can be presented in a disjointed way or with few (or no) evidence to support it, there should be a preliminary valuation of what is received and, if necessary, forwarding to the responsible areas, when it comes to more technical matters.[54] If there is sufficient materiality, the company can conduct an internal investigation to verify what was reported.[55]

The existence of internal protocols for analyzing complaints has both positive and negative aspects to highlight.[56]

Among the positives would be the possibility for the company to control what will be investigated before its reputation is damaged, for example. Furthermore, as will be seen in the following section, dedicated to the study of internal investigations, the company's knowledge of potential flaws in its internal controls will be crucial for enforcement agencies to validate the effectiveness of its compliance programme and for the company's cooperation, if it is in its interest, with public investigations.

On this point, there are scholars who believe that, when a crime is discovered within the private organisation, the company's role would be to report it to state agents, with the private entity only having the duty not to hinder the investigations carried out.[57]

Finally, another positive aspect would be that the proximity to the involved parties and the activities carried out makes it easier for the company to evaluate the irregularity and its possible causes.

The negative points, on the other hand, relate to the proximity of the whistleblower to the agent who may have committed the irregularity and, possibly, their subordination to him. In addition, if the company does not have solid internal policies, those responsible may not handle the matter in the most appropriate way, with possible threats and destruction of evidence, as in the famous case of Arthur Andersen and the documents related to the Enron fraud.

It is also important that the company maintains an open channel for third parties to report any irregularities they become aware of, whether through an internet page or even market announcements. Often, the absence of formal ties makes it easier for the whistleblower to present relevant information to the corporation.

In Brazil, the figure of the "good informant" recently gained prominence with the publication of the Anti-Crime Law (Law no. 13.964/2019), which made clear its source of inspiration in the USA, by determining the reward of up to 5% of the value recovered with the information provided. However, it is necessary to consider some points regarding the Brazilian reality and the challenges faced so that hotlines can effectively assist internal information flows and prevention policies.

---

[54] García-Moreno (2020, p. 273).

[55] Barbosa and Olivé (2019, p. 193).

[56] Ragués I Vallès (2006, pp. 156–157).

[57] Barbosa and Olivé (2019, p. 195).

Unlike the pragmatism that is characteristic of American society, informants in Brazil tend to be classified as traitors, which can hinder the use of these channels by company employees, in addition to the fact that our society would be defined by exaggerated individualism, with no culture of pressuring the culture of others (peer pressure).[58]

The Explanatory Memorandum of Bill no. 882/2019 highlighted the modification of the way evidence is currently produced, emphasising the difficulty in finding effective "witnesses to the [reported] fact" and explaining the reason why rewarded collaborations have gained relevance in favouring the criminal prosecution of serious corruption cases in Brazil. Unlike collaborators, the Explanatory Memorandum categorises informants as subjects who are not involved in crimes, but who wish to "merely assist the public power".

At the end of 2019, the figure of the whistleblower gained new delimitations in the Brazilian legal system with the changes made to the Dial-Denunciation Law (Law no. 13.608/2018) and the Law of Protection to Victims and Witnesses (Law no. 9.807/1999). The Anti-Crime Package, proposed by the Minister of Justice and Public Security and sanctioned by the President of Republic in 2019, brought two significant modifications to the figure of informants which were, in summary, (i) the obligation to install ombudsmen in public services, to receive information, ensuring the confidentiality of the informant, and (ii) the adoption of protection measures for whistleblowers, considering the financial, labour or even physical vulnerability of those who report an irregularity.[59]

The informant will be assured "full protection against retaliation and exemption from civil or criminal liability in relation to the report, except if the informant has knowingly presented false information or evidence".[60]

For Rodriguez, Saad-Diniz and Marin, the research carried out It is evident that whistleblowing channels are a distant reality for Brazilian companies: not only do few possess these *hotlines*, few reports of received complaints have also been recorded, which could be a reflection of[61]:

> (...) a certain conservatism of the national business sector, the anachronism of regulatory policy, and the disarticulation of *enforcement* authorities. Regrettably, the development of *compliance* solutions could not go beyond the formation of a self-referential industry, sustained by market discourses that impose a product through the often crude recourse to the fear of criminal intimidation.

In the USA, by comparison, the protection of *whistleblowers* does not take into account the motives that influenced them to report the irregularity, which, in the view of Ragués I Vallès, could be related to the marked individualism in American society, involving the prevention of workplace reprisals and the certainty that sanctions will be adopted against those who retaliate against their employees.[62]

---

[58] Rodríguez et al. (2020, p. 103).

[59] Souza (2020, pp. 46–47).

[60] Dezem and Souza (2020, p. 251).

[61] Rodríguez et al. (2020, p. 91).

[62] Ragués I Vallès (2006, pp. 23–27).

Considering the complexity of business activities and the lack of state capacity to monitor and supervise ever-larger and globally dispersed companies, the way in which the internal organisation decides to deal with the information received will be crucial in proving that the implemented programme genuinely aims to mitigate risks and keep activities within permitted limits.

The figure of the *whistleblowers* is not easily defined; some liken them to informers and traitors, while others will see them as heroes, without whom major economic scandals would never be uncovered. More than figures laden with moral convictions, the aim of the communications made by *whistleblowers* should be to report irregularities identified in the daily life of the company, so that it is possible to cease the practice, if necessary, and correct the failures that gave rise to them, preventing their repetition.

In this sense, the way in which the whistleblowing channel is presented to employees will be decisive for its success or, conversely, its symbolic use.

A criticism made regarding the regulation of whistleblower protection is that, although much emphasise is placed on its importance, no strategy has been presented on how to effectively protect them from potential retaliations that may arise and how to sanction those who persecute an employee after the communication of potential irregularities.[63] One can, in this regard, take as an example the protections assured in Brazil by Law No. 9.807/1999,[64] in addition to others such as job security in the face of arbitrary dismissals, withdrawal of benefits, negative merit evaluations, and other forms of persecution.[65]

However, the way in which such protections will be assured and the perpetrators punished is linked to case-by-case analyses. The lack of normative provision also affects the potential (since it is not mandatory) payment of a reward to the informant for the information provided.[66]

There is also a phenomenon that is the result of the policy of cooperation between public and private agents that will be analysed in greater depth later in this research.

---

[63] Rodríguez et al. (2020, p. 98).

[64] "*Art. 7 ° of law no. 9.807/1999 - The programmes* [special protection for victims and threatened witnesses] *include, among others, the following measures, applicable separately or cumulatively for the benefit of the protected person, according to the severity and circumstances of each case: I - security at residence, including telecommunications control; II - escort and safety during travel from the residence, including for work purposes or for giving testimonies; III - relocation or temporary accommodation in a place compatible with protection; IV - preservation of identity, image and personal data; V - monthly financial aid to cover necessary expenses for individual or family subsistence, in case the protected person is unable to carry out regular work or there is no source of income; VI - temporary suspension of functional activities, without prejudice to their respective earnings or advantages, when a public servant or military; VII - social, medical and psychological support and assistance; VIII - confidentiality regarding the acts performed due to the granted protection; IX - support from the programme's executing body for the fulfilment of civil and administrative obligations that require personal attendance. Single paragraph. The monthly financial aid will have a cap set by the deliberative council at the beginning of each financial year*".

[65] Dezem and Souza (2020, p. 251).

[66] Dezem and Souza (2020, p. 251).

With the aim of collaborating with as much information as possible in the investigations conducted by the prosecuting bodies and thus ensuring a possible reduction of sanctions, companies may practice what Laufer classifies as *reverse whistleblowing*, which occurs when the company identifies certain employees as responsible for the irregularity and offers evidence against them in exchange for leniency or a possible amnesty, in the American context, for the legal entity (*trading favors*).[67]

The criticism made by Laufer is that the need to make agreements with the public power would encourage this practice, since the legal entity can use the individual as a strategy to assert that the failure was isolated and not the result of structural problems in its internal controls. The scapegoats (*scapegoating*) can be consensual, when there is an agreement between, usually, more senior employees or the high administration, who will be "*remunerated*" to take responsibility for the irregularity, or non-consensual, which will occur when an employee not necessarily guilty is blamed in place of the legal entity.[68]

Considering the fact that public bodies often fail to grasp the potential severity of corporate disorganisation, the information received from corporations will be used as a benchmark in accusations.

Finally, another avenue for obtaining internal information is through exit interviews. Often, hierarchy, corporate ties, or even personal relationships can prevent an employee from reporting any improper conduct they may have encountered or become aware of. In this regard, interviews conducted when an employee is no longer associated with the company can be of great importance for *compliance.*

Summarising the role of whistleblowing channels within compliance structures, they represent a significant source of information for the company, which should have its structures well explained so that employees trust in reporting any irregularities they become aware of in the course of their work. This tool also requires the establishment of internal procedures for receiving, analysing, and investigating information, with firm measures against retaliation of *whistleblowers* and regular training so that *hotlines* are known to their employees, and their proper use aids the development of internal controls.

However, it is always necessary to emphasise that the aim of internal channels is not to create a climate of surveillance and denunciation within the company, as this would not be an indicator of efficiency, but of the implementation of a weak organisational culture.

3.6 Corporate Investigations

One of the most delicate aspects of *compliance* policies is corporate investigations, the applicable rules, whether they are closer to the Code of Criminal Procedure or to a private corporate logic, who would be responsible for their implementation

---

[67] Laufer (2002, p. 648).

[68] Laufer (2002, p. 649).

and what limits the legal entity should observe, especially considering that, during the investigations, there may be a weighing of the intended objectives against the fundamental rights of workers.

What reasons might lead a company to conduct internal investigations? Some examples can be given, such as the need to obtain information about a particular conduct, which may even enable it to be stopped; it may also aim to determine a strategy for handling a case in which the company finds itself involved, or even to have more information to negotiate a deal with the *enforcement* agencies.

Seen as a way to give greater agility and effectiveness to public investigations, especially as they do not require authorisations and judicial cooperation agreements,[69] internal inquiries occupy a significant place within *compliance* programmes, as they can be used to uncover any irregularities, hitherto unknown, or to investigate information received through the information channels provided. Far from being an indication, solely, that the *compliance* programme has failed, internal investigations seek to analyse the reported occurrence and assist the company in determining new policies that will prevent the problem from recurring in the future.

There are, in the doctrine, different classifications about the objectives sought with corporate investigations and also about how they are initiated.

In a first classification, based on the origin of the demand, two forms can be highlighted: (i) the *pre-judicial investigations*, which are those initiated from indications of the commission of crimes, usually through information received in the internal whistleblowing channels (*whistleblower*), or (ii) *para-judicial investigations*, that is, those conducted under the requirement of authorities for clarification of a specific fact.[70]

Within a perception of corporate social responsibility and with the latest ESG policies, corporations are expected to keep their activities and risks under control. However, the issue takes on another dimension when the internal activities implemented by the corporation are used against it in administrative proceedings or in searches for the accountability of its managers and representatives.

Add to this the lack of standards for valuing the efforts made by private entities, and we are faced with a scenario of legal uncertainty and disparate treatment by the *enforcement* agencies.

As verified in regulatory frameworks, obligated agents need, based on applicable regulations, to implement sufficient internal controls that allow their activity to remain within the risks permitted for each economic sector. For example, Law No. 9,613/98 provides, in its articles 9 to 12, that certain private agents should implement prevention duties and, especially, collaboration in their agendas.

The Anti-Corruption Law, in turn, establishes in its article 7 which elements will be taken into account at the time of applying the sanction and, among them, clause VII brings "the cooperation of the legal entity in the investigation of infractions".

In terms of *compliance, it can be argued that internal investigations would constitute a duty of companies, as they tend to ensure that the activities performed will*

---

[69] Nieto Martín (2019, p. 39).

[70] Montiel (2013, p. 261).

remain within the bounds of legality or even detect problems in the business organisation. Another view is that companies should prevent irregularities, but not implement efforts to detect and sanction employees, leaving investigations as a factual duty of companies that will seek to mitigate any sanctions, if necessary, by presenting to public bodies the efforts and documents produced.[71]

Regardless of the interpretation followed, the company's cooperation with the investigations carried out by the prosecution bodies, providing information and documents obtained through their internal efforts, receives significant attention from the regulator. Thus, defining the scope of the internal investigation will be the main moment for the focus of the due diligence to be sufficient to elucidate the necessary information.

Within the definition, there will be the duration period, which areas are involved, the mapping of information sources and the expected outcomes. In this sense, it is not feasible to have several points of analysis, considering the necessary attention for each of them, as well as the potential future need for *disclosure.* It is also important to define in advance points such as the frequency of reports on the results of the investigations, where the resources will come from, keeping in mind the need for independence and impartiality.

It is possible to make a comparative analysis with the American guidelines which, as verified, have directly influenced the criminal policy implemented in Brazil.

In the Thompson Memorandum, published by the DOJ in 2003, the American agency begins the document stating that, with the criminal prosecution work implemented by the government, companies had internalised the importance of self-regulation, especially since industry participants had been convicted.[72] According to the Memorandum, the attribution of responsibility to the legal entity would be determined discretionarily by the prosecutor, after analysing the need for sanctions based on criteria learnt from the DOJ's experience.

In this context, important points to be considered are:

(i) the nature and seriousness of the irregularity committed;
(ii) the risk to the public and to the market as a whole (collateral damage caused);
(iii) the spread of the improper practice within the company's activities;
(iv) the company's history ("*it is expected for the corporation to learn from its mistakes*");
(v) the existence of *compliance* programmes and internal controls (it is highlighted in the Thompson Memorandum that, at the time, there were no pre-established criteria that could determine the efficiency of the established controls, which is why it would be up to the prosecutor to make a case-by-case analysis, considering the reality presented by the company and the needs and risks of the market in which it is inserted);

[71] Montiel (2013, pp. 263–264).

[72] U.S. Department of Justice. Office of the Deputy Attorney General. *Principles of Federal Prosecution of Business Organizations.* Jan./2003.

(vi) the company's timeliness in presenting evidence of the irregularity and its willingness to cooperate with the investigations, recognising the difficulty of state agents in overcoming the complex corporate obstacles;
(vii) adequacy and necessity of eventual prosecution of individuals and
(viii) adequacy of alternative measures and corrections implemented by the company (evidence of the application of internal sanctions, especially if the irregularity involves higher positions).

The Thompson Memorandum thus indicates that, in the early 2000s, the DOJ focused on acting through the accountability of legal entities, although it highlighted that sanctions on the company would not exempt natural persons involved in the identified irregularities from responsibility.

In 2015, after many criticisms not only about companies *too big to fail*, but also about administrators *too big to jail*, new guidance is published with the so-called Yates Memorandum, which aimed at the civil and criminal prosecution of individuals who committed irregularities in the business sphere. The DOJ, recognising the difficulty in establishing responsibilities in the face of the complexity of corporate structures, began to encourage legal entities to cooperate with public agents, delivering all the evidence they have about illegal acts committed by their representatives.[73] This information would be crucial for the acceptance, by the prosecution bodies, of the agreements on the table.

In September 2022, however, the so-called Monaco Memorandum was published, which begins with the assertion that an effective *enforcement* model would be one that does not allow the existence of two rights in the USA, one for corporations and their executives and another for the rest of *America.* The document highlights the importance of proactive action by corporations, in reporting any irregularities they become aware of, being also timely and well-founded, with special attention to the provision of evidence that ensures the individualisation of responsibilities, whether these documents are obtained domestically or internationally (it is pointed out that this would tend to score points additional positives with the regulator, given the complexity of obtaining evidence in subsidiaries or foreign companies).

The Memorandum highlights the importance of international cooperation between jurisdictions, considering that corporate delinquency can take on different forms in various countries. Identifying regulatory synergies would therefore be strategic to ensure effective *enforcement* against individuals and corporations.

Furthermore, within the analysis carried out by American prosecutors, the company's history should be considered, including all scenarios and contexts (civil, regulatory, and criminal). Such antecedents would allow for the verification of the effectiveness of the *compliance* programme and the measurement of whether the changes implemented internally had the expected effects or if the company's structural disorganisation was maintained. At this point, it would be up to the State to also

[73] U.S. Department of Justice. Office of the Deputy Attorney General. *Individual Accountability for Corporate Wrongdoing*. Sep./2015.

verify the recidivism of the individuals involved, in order to prove whether the previously applied sanctions were sufficient or if the corporate culture oriented towards improper practices and conduct indicated a problematic and uncorrected root cause.

Drawing a parallel with Latin American regulations, the provision brought by the Chilean Law can be cited, which established that in the event of criminal liability of legal entities, the timely cooperation of companies and their representatives will be considered a mitigating circumstance for the dosimetry of the penalty eventually applicable (article 6).

In Brazil, Decree No. 8,240/2015 established, as one of the criteria for the celebration of leniency agreements with the public power, that companies cooperate *fully and permanently* with the investigations, presenting documents and information that prove and assist in the investigation of the harmful act analysed.

In this context of collaboration with the State, in order to obtain documents and information necessary for potential mitigation of their sanctions, companies need to have appropriate internal procedures that allow them to obtain the necessary material to assess their situation and, consequently, define the best strategy to be followed.

From the companies' perspective, the investigation function tends to bring new risks that need to be considered.[74] The first is related to the risk of possible liability for the insufficiency of what is put into practice and how state bodies tend to evaluate the efforts made.

The second highlighted risk is related to possible violations of the fundamental rights of their employees. As it is a *reactive tool*,[75] it is necessary that there are protocols to be followed by those internally responsible for the investigations, in order to avoid possible abuses. Transparency with those involved is fundamental to reject any flaws in the conduct of internal investigations.

From the perspective of strategy definition, each step must be conducted with caution, considering that the information obtained may be used later in legal proceedings. The existence of a so-called "*Corporate Miranda*" linked to employees who find themselves involved in internal investigations is even mentioned.[76]

In this sense, the criteria and procedures of internal investigations should be provided for in the *compliance* programme, also because the employee's cooperation can be seen as a contractual duty enforceable by the employer which, in some cases, may come as an unpleasant surprise if not previously communicated. There is an understanding that investigations carried out by the company constitute employment practice and, therefore, are private, not needing to follow the rules provided for in the Code of Criminal Procedure, just ensure that the procedures are disclosed transparently, especially considering the risk of legal challenges.[77]

The interdisciplinary nature of *compliance* is present when the importance of information security policies is highlighted: employees must be aware that their computers and other equipment provided by the company are subject to monitoring.

---

[74] Feldens and Diettrich (2016, p. 49).

[75] Nieto Martín (2019, p. 294).

[76] Nieto Martín (2019, p. 315).

[77] Moosmayer (2013, pp. 140) and following.

In conducting the investigations, those in charge will define the criteria for analysing the information and how they will be examined within the proposed objectives.

At this point, it is necessary to highlight the difference between the functions of internal audit and the role of internal investigators: in the first case, the function will be to verify the functioning of the system, while the latter have a reactive character, that is, they will act based on prior knowledge that there is, at least, a suspicion of irregularity.[78]

Initially, one can analyze what incentives will influence the decision of companies to implement efforts for the conduct of internal investigations. Many authors question what has been conventionally called the *privatisation* of the State's persecutory functions. Aware of its inability to deal with structures in the face of complex corporate structures and constantly changing economic activities, the State delegates to private entities the responsibility for preventing irregularities, as well as being able to provide all necessary information for potential attribution of liability.[79]

After the phase of analysing and reviewing corporate documents is completed, the internal investigation can move to the interview phase with those who may, in some way, be involved with the irregularity. Here, it is important that the investigators are familiar with the company's organisational chart, in order to structure and conduct the interviews more logically.

The suspects, their direct supervisors, and colleagues will be interviewed with the aim of discussing points related to the investigation within its context.

At this point, it is important to pay attention to the fact that companies, as private agents, should not make accusations or coerce their employees, keeping the dealings within the procedures provided for in internal policies. In addition, transparency is fundamental: while respecting the necessary confidentiality and secrecy, the interviewees should know the reason why they are participating in that diligence.

It is recommended that interviews be conducted in person to avoid possible phone interceptions and ensure that investigators have close contact with the interviewees' reactions, which can favour the obtaining of relevant information. Just as corporate governance is discussed, it is necessary to highlight the importance of so-called investigation governance, establishing limits and guidelines, since the actions and diligences carried out may conflict with the fundamental rights of their employees.

It is important that the employee who participates as a witness or as an accused is aware of the conflicts of interest related to the situation, as well as the fact that they are not protected by that legal representative, since, at that moment, the lawyer is

[78] Nieto Martín (2019, p. 294).

[79] On this subject, it is interesting to point out the criticisms brought in the North American context where the privatization of prosecutorial functions has encompassed not only investigations, but in some US cities the very activity of prosecution. With the objectives of bringing greater efficiency to the criminal system and, primarily, reducing costs, law firms are hired, with hourly remuneration, by the government to conduct investigations, accuse individuals and determine whether agreements will be made or not with the accused. Considering the costs attributed to public employees, in certain municipalities where there is no significant incidence of crimes, the State understands that it is not necessary to maintain a prosecutor allocated, just the hiring of law firms for the prosecutorial functions. Fairfax Jr (2010, pp. 266–282). On the subject, Maroto Calatayud (2008).

representing the legal entity and, if it is in the employee's interest, they may appear with a lawyer appointed by them. In American doctrine, this practice became known as the *Upjohn Warning*, which stipulates that the employee should be previously informed about the objectives of the interview and that the information discussed there can, if it is in the company's interest, be disclosed to regulatory bodies.

In the USA, there is strong jurisprudence to protect the information obtained by legal representatives, with some criteria having been established that must be observed. In the case of *Upjohn v. United States*, it was determined that the privilege of confidentiality would apply, in summary, (i) to the communicated information that was necessary for legal advice; (ii) the communications were related to the scope of the employee's work in the company; (iii) the employee was aware that the shared information would be used by the company, if necessary; and (iv) the company's intention was to keep the information confidential.[80]

In summary, it can be said that the existing confidentiality, with regard to the information obtained in the interviews, will be of the company and not of the interviewees, which can open space for ethical challenges.[81] Therefore, it will be up to the lawyer or whoever plays the role of investigator to make it clear, preferably in writing, that the interviewee understood and consented that the information obtained could be published by the company if it was in its interest.

There is an understanding in the doctrine that, at first, while the analysis is restricted to the company, it can be assumed that, for private contractual reasons, the employee would have the duty to cooperate with the investigations conducted internally, while the requirement would have a new configuration from the moment it is known that the information will be used in criminal proceedings.[82] However, considering the necessary prior execution of the scope of the investigation and its possible developments, any interview conducted with employees, notwithstanding the existing contractual duty, should be preceded by explanations that it is a corporate diligence and that it is up to the employee to participate alone or hire a lawyer to accompany them.

Investigations can be carried out within the financial scope of corporations and, for this, it is necessary to have the participation of specialised experts and, if necessary, technology companies responsible for extracting the documents. The analysis will be carried out on payment vouchers, receipts and invoices, records, and internal accounting balances.

At the end of the internal investigations, it is essential that the final report, in addition to reporting the facts found, evaluates the *compliance* programme and what changes are necessary to prevent, if applicable, new irregularities from occurring or repeating.

As for the content of the reports, there would be some essential items involved:

(i) summary of the initial allegations that initiated the investigation;

[80] Ramm (2018, p. 304).

[81] Dunst and Chirlin (2009, p. 1).

[82] Montiel (2013, p. 272).

(ii) the scope of the conducted investigation;
(iii) the adopted methodology;
(iv) the description of the facts analyzed;
(v) the legal analysis of the findings and, finally,
(vi) the proposed remediation measures.

The language of the report should be clear, direct, impartial, and focused on identifying the main points raised in the investigation conducted.

Among the proposed remediation measures, there will be suggestions aimed at improving what was analysed by the responsible team, such as, for example, conducting training on internal policies; the review or supplementation of existing internal rules; improving the procedures of *due diligence* with respect to third parties; dismissal of employees, with or without just cause (which will require a joint analysis with the internal legal team, considering possible litigation of the issue) and, if necessary, the recommendation of improvements in internal controls.

The improvements will be important to demonstrate that the company, aware of any weaknesses in its *compliance* programme, is willing to invest and stay organised internally.

In addition to demonstrating efforts to regulatory bodies, the modifications will show employees that there is effectiveness and seriousness in the way the information received is handled by the corporation, whether through the assurance of maintaining confidentiality about who reported an irregularity or even by the way it will be handled internally, with detailed analysis and *enforcement* measures applied, if applicable.

3.6.1 Duty to Report to Regulatory Bodies

Upon concluding internal investigations, the company may or may not discover that violations have been perpetrated by its representatives. If so, the next step will be to internally analyse the need to report the irregularities to the regulatory bodies or if it would be sufficient to implement the remediation measures.

The case involving the Madero group, referenced below, highlights the complexity surrounding the disclosure of information to regulatory bodies. If the company considers the positive aspects of disclosing the results of its investigations to the State, it could consider the expected reduction in fines, since its cooperation will result in more lenient treatment by the authorities; moreover, as it was responsible for conducting the investigations, the company has greater control over what will be disclosed, theoretically managing the effects on its reputation.

The negative points, however, involve a complex process of collaboration with regulatory bodies and all the legal uncertainty that permeates this reality.

Among the points of attention that should be considered are the possible weaknesses identified by the investigations. For example, if the investigation originated from an internal complaint, the *whistleblower* may understand that the disclosure of information to the competent bodies should be done obligatorily and, if the company does not opt for this path, it may give the impression that the *compliance* did not take the necessary measures.

The next step of the informant may be to seek external communication channels (*external whistleblower*), which would deprive the company of the advantages of being the one to report the irregularity. As Isabel Franco highlights, "*the worst situation in which the company can find itself is to learn of facts from the authorities that it did not even imagine were happening within its premises*".[83]

Conducting processes in foreign jurisdictions also constitutes a risk to be considered, especially in the era of almost total monitoring. The case of Embraer, e.g., highlights this risk, given that the investigations in Brazil arose after communication from American entities. The extraterritorial reach of norms, such as *FCPA* and *Bribery Act*, reinforces the company's analysis to check risks related to foreign jurisdictions.

It should be noted that the decision to report an irregularity of which it becomes aware is a prerogative of the company, and it cannot be prejudiced for not presenting evidence that could potentially incriminate it.[84] The company cannot be obliged to contribute to its own accusation.[85]

It was previously studied that the State, aware of the informational disadvantage it is exposed to, the complexity of the analysis it would face if it had to check each of the corporate structures and their multitude of documentation, chooses to delegate to private entities the task of investigating any identified irregularities.[86] Some of the criticisms of the model of joint action between public and private entities are related to the confusion between the limits of action of each side and the definition of roles in this context.

From the moment the State acknowledges its inability to access all information related to the company, an opportunity is created for the company to construct a more favourable narrative, either by selecting the evidence that will be submitted or even by directing individual criminal charges against previously determined subjects.[87] This concern should already exist when the company initiates internal investigations, at which point it weighs the risk associated with each of its objectives and the consequent duties of *disclosure.*

On the other hand, some believe that the State would take advantage of the company's duty to cooperate to gain access to evidence that would not be legally obtained if the investigation was not conducted internally by the employer who, as observed, may not respect all the fundamental rights of its workers.

Finally, the importance of confidentiality within private investigations should be emphasised, whether in relation to those involved or even with the company's information (such as industrial and commercial secrets) that may be disclosed.[88]

---

[83] Franco (2020, p. 198).

[84] Costa and Araújo (2014, p. 228).

[85] Nieto Martín (2013, p. 47).

[86] Griffin (2011, p. 112).

[87] Griffin (2011, p. 114).

[88] Moosmayer (2013, p. 142).

What can be observed is that the company faces a delicate dilemma when considering whether or not to present the results of its internal investigations to public bodies. In this regard, an interesting case to mention is that of Ralph Lauren, regarding the accusation of involvement in the payment of bribes in Argentina.

After receiving a complaint through the company's internal channels, it was discovered that, over a four-year period (2005 to 2009), bribes had been paid to Argentine customs agents with the aim of ensuring the importation of goods without bureaucracy or inspections that could delay procedures.[89] In addition to the improper payments, which reached about US$600,000, various gifts from the brand were identified as being sent to Argentine officials.[90]

Upon reporting its investigations to the DOJ, Ralph Lauren had already implemented various changes and improvements in its internal controls, such as, for example, (i) the translation of its anti-corruption policies; (ii) due diligence applied to third parties; (iii) the modernisation of its rules on gifts and commissions; (iv) implementation of new face-to-face anti-corruption training; and also (v) conducting risk assessments according to the countries in which it maintained operations, such as Italy and Japan.[91] These efforts demonstrated to the DOJ that the company had effectively committed to the development of effective internal programmes, which resulted in low financial sanctions.

More than the concern with a possible formal accountability of the company before the prosecuting bodies, the relevant reputational aspect should be highlighted. Considering the change in the profile of consumers, more concerned with issues such as sustainability and transparency, it can be said that, with the prevention measures and improvements adopted by the company, there was also concern with the *immaterial aspect* of business activity.[92]

The absence of regulation on the subject of corporate investigations, as well as the legal uncertainty identified in negotiations with the State, will make it difficult to weigh the negative and positive aspects of the option to report internally discovered irregularities. Factors such as *self-reporting*, collaboration with public investigations, and the remedial measures implemented by companies should have their valuation determined in a more transparent way by regulatory bodies.[93]

The lack of evaluation parameters on the part of the State regarding the information presented by companies can weaken the self-regulation environment, because without knowing how their conduct will be evaluated, private entities may choose not to report discovered irregularities, especially if they verify that the problem was isolated and with little chance of being discovered.[94]

Add to this the fact that the evaluation of their collaboration will involve the company's reality, pre- and post-irregularity. In this sense, some considerations

---

[89] Reilly (2014, pp. 4–6).

[90] Ferreira and Okada (2020, p. 127).

[91] Reilly (2014, pp. 7–10).

[92] Ferreira and Okada (2020, p. 129).

[93] Reilly (2014, pp. 44–45).

[94] Reilly (2014, pp. 25–29).

will be part of the company's decision chain, such as reputational impact, which will be reflected in the share prices, if applicable, or even the loss of credibility with customers.[95] Like everything in business activity, the decision to report its irregularities will be a *trade-off* of difficult solution.

3.6.2 Defensive Investigations

In some cases, the legal entity may not be aware of the irregularities committed by its representatives, needing to conduct its own investigations defensively with the aim, for example, of demonstrating that the irregular practice constituted a one-off conduct, having implemented effective internal controls at the macro-managerial level.

Furthermore, investigations may form part of internal policies for detecting irregularities and will be requested preventively by the legal entity. The topic of defensive investigations opens a wide range of subjects that deserve discussion, albeit briefly, considering their complexity and importance.

In this context, Provision No. 188/2018, published by the Brazilian Bar Association (OAB), aimed to regulate the role of the lawyer in the occurrence of investigative diligences aimed at instructing administrative and judicial procedures. This Provision defines defensive investigation, through its Article 1, as follows:

> Article 1. Defensive investigation is understood as the complex of investigative activities carried out by the lawyer, with or without the assistance of a technical consultant or other legally qualified professionals, at any stage of criminal prosecution, procedure or degree of jurisdiction, aiming at obtaining elements of evidence intended for the constitution of a lawful evidentiary collection, for the protection of the rights of their client.

Defensive investigation, according to the regulation, can be carried out at any time during a process, whether for the preparation of defence pieces or to bring relevant corroborative elements for the execution of leniency or plea-bargain agreements with regulatory bodies.

Provision 188/2018 emphasises that the information obtained in the context of a defensive investigation must be kept confidential by the lawyer, and should protect "*the dignity, privacy, intimacy and other individual rights and guarantees of the people involved*" (Article 5). Although the legal representative has no obligation to report the information obtained, they can only do so with prior authorisation from the client (Article 6).

Furthermore, the regulation brings interesting regulation to defensive investigations and legal security for the professionals responsible for them. Considering the Brazilian reality and the true—and not yet entirely overcome—inquisitorial culture

---

[95] Reilly (2014, pp. 15–22).

that permeates criminal proceedings, strengthening the investigations carried out by the defence constitutes a significant step in the challenge of effectively ensuring parity of arms in the criminal procedural sphere.

Similarly, it can be argued that defensive investigation strengthens due process, as it will impact the quality and quantity of evidence that will be part of the process.[96]

It should be noted, however, that there is a cultural barrier to be overcome in the Brazilian reality, as there is a tendency to give greater value and relevance to the evidence produced by the prosecution, as if the defensive evidence, in some way, were intended only to disrupt the process and confuse the judge. On the other hand, the defendant who does not cooperate is also seen as an obstacle to the sought-after speed.

To illustrate the risks and subtlety of the topic, one can cite the case of the law firm *Jones Day* in Germany. When the scandal of manipulation of pollutant emitters involving automotive companies arose, the American firm was hired to conduct internal investigations at Volkswagen S.A. The Public Prosecutor's Office filed a search and seizure request at the law firm, which was granted by the German Constitutional Court on the grounds that the documents obtained in the investigation, carried out prior to the process, would not be protected by confidentiality.[97]

Another interesting case involves the *Serious Fraud Office* (SFO) and the company Eurasian Natural Resources Corporation (ENRC), responsible for the internal investigation of one of its subsidiaries, located in Kazakhstan, after receiving anonymous reports of corruption.[98]

At first instance, it was decided that the documents would not enjoy professional protection, as they were produced prior to the existence of the judicial process. According to the interpretation of the *High Court*, confidentiality would be applicable to materials that were used in adversarial litigation, not for procedures carried out for preventive purposes.

However, there was no evidence to show that ENRC was anticipating materials for a possible judicial process.[99] On appeal, the *Court of Appeal,* however, understood exactly the opposite, that is, that the company's measures were taken with a focus on a future litigation perspective, for which reason its protection would be appropriate. Thus, in the United Kingdom, the confidentiality of information covers documents that contain some analysis, contribution or legal advice that should be protected; it is not enough to expect that the documents will be used in future judicial litigation.[100]

---

[96] Baldan (2019, p. 9).

[97] Teixeira and Wehrs (2020).

[98] Teixeira and Wehrs (2020).

[99] Ramm (2018, p. 310).

[100] Ramm (2018, pp. 310–311).

In the U.S. context, considering the need to collaborate with criminal prosecution agents ("*Corporate America as an arm of law enforcement*"), the requirement, although not always public, that companies waive rights such as the non-self-incrimination and confidentiality in exchange for a state policy of legal efficiency.[101]

In Brazil, the activity of investigation by private agents tends to encounter a culture in which judges already have a formed hypothesis, with the prosecution providing evidence that validates and corroborates what has already been defined. In this context, defensive investigations aim to create new hypotheses that seek to alternatively explain the facts and present elements that dismiss unwanted hypotheses.

The legal uncertainty present in the professional confidentiality of lawyers constitutes a serious problem in the duties of prevention and collaboration that are required of private entities. From the moment the company fears that potential internal investigations may be used against it in a possible legal process, efforts to discover the facts tend to decrease.

The legal system, while offering incentives for companies to cooperate with state investigations, must also ensure that they are not, in reality, providing evidence against themselves.[102]

3.7 Agreements with the Public Authority

At the beginning of the text, we discussed how criminal law is interconnecting with economics as a validator of the dominant structure through symbolic norms, short-term focused and inefficient.[103] The symbolism becomes more evident when we consider the difficulty in protecting the business sphere, given the complex corporate structures and economic irregularities.

These pose a challenge to enforcement agencies, given the impasses found to define and assign individual criminal responsibilities without becoming objective (for example, punishing someone for the position held within the business hierarchy). Furthermore, the long years of investigations and trials, as well as the necessary compensation for damages caused, demand a speed greater than that existing in the criminal process.

In this context, it is asserted that the participation of the corporations themselves in the criminal process will be determinant for the success of the investigations, since the State would have limited capacity to decipher the internal business mysteries. This logic has already been perceived in the administrative sphere, where complex infractions and the strengthening of procedural guarantees have increased the costs

[101] Laufer (2002, p. 651).

[102] Ramm (2018, pp. 319–320).

[103] Silva Sánchez (2004, pp. 39) and ss.

of the State to execute its procedural functions, as well as having reduced the chances of State success in the accusations.[104]

"The process is the punishment": with this phrase, which conveys the idea that the process is in itself a sanction, Nieto Martín justifies the reasons why procedural incentives become attractive to legal entities and their administrators who, in order to avoid financial and reputational losses, make agreements with public bodies to terminate ongoing processes or investigations.[105]

Agreements with the Public Authority can be made by both individuals and legal entities. In this context, there is a clear influence of plea bargaining institutions and DPAs and NPAs (Non-prosecution Agreement) widely practiced in the common law system, especially in the USA.

At first, the negotiation logic seems strange to the structures of Brazilian Criminal Law, if we think about the need to implement bargaining strategies, the recent availability of public interest, as well as the multiplicity of bodies with which negotiations must be established.[106] Add to this the fact that, in the USA, a confession is sufficient to substantiate a conviction, whereas here, it constitutes one of the elements of proof.[107]

In addition, the way agreements have been conducted by prosecuting bodies in the so-called Operation Car Wash causes strangeness to those who still imagine themselves in a democratic state of law. We do not intend to address all the complexity related to the proposition of agreements by imprisoned defendants, but if the normative requirements of voluntariness and the necessary corroboration of information with more corroborative elements are considered, it will be difficult not to disagree with the customary practice that has been established in Brazil.

The violation of individual rights is also pointed out in the North American context, where threats made by prosecuting bodies are denounced, through the imposition of significant penalties as ways to "convince" the accused to admit guilt for crimes attributed to them, even if they know themselves to be innocent.

Another difference between the Brazilian figure of the informer and the practice of the *plea bargain* is that in the latter there is an admission of guilt, while in the former, the informer's statements involve obtaining information (and evidence) about the involvement of third parties in criminal structures.[108] As pointed out in the case of *whistleblowers*, the role of informers, who here are co-authors of crimes and not just observers as in the previous figure, is viewed with considerable caution. If ethical and moral aspects are considered, the behaviour of the informer can be seen as disloyal or even motivated by false reasons, aimed solely and exclusively at obtaining procedural advantages.[109]

---

[104] Marrara (2015, p. 511).

[105] Nieto Martín (2019, p. 323).

[106] Tojal and Tamasaukas (2020, pp. 128–129).

[107] Matos (2018, p. 3).

[108] Zilli (2017).

[109] Matos (2018, p. 4).

Although they gained prominence with the mega-operation of Lava Jato, negotiation practices with prosecution bodies are not recent, but date back to the 90s of the last century, when the Brazilian Heinous Crimes Law (Law No. 8.072/1990) determined, in a utilitarian way, the provision of plea-bargaining for those who had information that could result in the release of the kidnapped person.[110]

In 2013, with the Brazilian Criminal Organisations Law (Law No. 12.850/2013), the instrument of plea bargaining was better detailed, providing for the reduction of sentence or even judicial pardon to the subject who collaborated effectively and voluntarily with the authorities.[111] The norm established what requirements would be necessary for the contribution to be considered effective, such as, for example, the identification of co-authors, the structures of the criminal organisation, as well as the total or partial recovery of the proceeds of the infractions committed.

The leniency agreements signed with legal entities, in turn, arise in the competitive sphere and were better regulated by Law No. 12.529/2011. This norm proves to be the most complete when it comes to the negotiation route, providing for the possibility of celebrating the agreement in the pre-procedural phase and also the so-called leniency *plus*, which will occur when there is a second agreement signed between the individual and the State, but based on a new infraction, hitherto unknown.[112]

As Silveira asserts, it is a hybrid figure, which involves the administrative and criminal spheres, and has become a "*fundamental pillar of the National Policy for the protection of economic order*".[113]

Under the terms of article 86, *caput*, of the aforementioned norm, CADE may enter into a leniency agreement, with the extinction of punitive action by the public administration or the reduction of the penalty, "*with individuals and legal entities that are authors of an infraction to the economic order, provided they effectively collaborate with the investigations and the administrative process*". The requirements for the agreement consist in that the information provided allows the identification of the other parties involved in the infraction and the obtaining of information and documents that assist in the investigations.

Leniency agreements can be categorised as a "*providing of evidence [by the private agent] in exchange for the mitigation of punishment or even its extinction*".[114] As Marrara asserts, lenient will be the State, in the figure of the public entity that mitigates

---

[110] Silveira (2014, p. 17).

[111] "*Art. 4 The judge may, at the request of the parties, grant judicial pardon, reduce by up to 2/3 (two thirds) the custodial sentence or replace it with restrictive rights for those who have effectively and voluntarily collaborated with the investigation and the criminal process, provided that this collaboration results in one or more of the following outcomes: I - the identification of the other co-authors and participants of the criminal organisation and the criminal offences they committed; II - the revelation of the hierarchical structure and division of tasks of the criminal organisation; III - the prevention of criminal offences resulting from the activities of the criminal organisation; IV - the total or partial recovery of the product or profit of the criminal offences committed by the criminal organisation; V - the location of any victim with their physical integrity preserved*".

[112] Marrara (2015, p. 516).

[113] Silveira (2014, pp. 19) and following.

[114] Marrara (2015, p. 512).

the exercise of its punitive power, while the individual will be the beneficiary of leniency, the one who offers his contribution.[115]

Although there is provision for mitigation or even absence of sanction in the scope of the competition norm, seen as a positive judgement of the participation of the private agent, the state's objective with the agreements signed is to obtain evidence that allows the instruction of the administrative process and the punishment of the other parties involved.[116]

The discussion about the responsibility of corporations for infractions resulting from the lack of internal organisation has been gaining prominence in Brazil in recent times, especially with all the regulatory structure that orbits the demands for internal controls and *compliance* programmes, whose objective, for many, is just to keep business activity within the allowed risks.

Saad-Diniz divides into five phases the evolution of the movements that led to the development of criminal policy aimed at attributing responsibilities to collective entities[117]:

(i) regulatory porosity, where initially there would be no defined strategy on how to approach the internal disarray that would give room for the commission of infractions within the business sphere;
(ii) ambiguity, considering the historical complicity of major icons of capitalism with totalitarian regimes;
(iii) post-War polarity, characterised by the morality resulting from the *Watergate* scandal, as we previously noted, with the creation of the FCPA and the linking of corporate criminal liability to the development of an ethical business culture;
(iv) market integration and intensification of capital and people flows, generating an alignment of expectations and conduct standards, as was clear in the criminal policy related to international movements for money laundering prevention and anti-corruption and, finally,
(v) the role of regulation which, aware of the insufficiency of traditional legal models, needs to deal with environments of enormous complexity, informational asymmetry and organised irresponsibility.

The Brazilian Anti-Corruption Law, that is, the aforementioned Law No. 12.846/2013, introduced the provision of two new hypotheses for leniency agreements: for corrupt practices and for those related to the Procurement Law (at the time, Law No. 8.666/1993).

The influence of the procedures adopted in competition infractions[118] is clear. The anti-corruption norm strengthened the participation of companies, encouraging internal controls which, if well implemented, would tend to discover more evidence of irregularities committed within the corporate sphere, resulting in the discretionary presentation of this information to public bodies.

---

[115] Marrara (2015, p. 512).

[116] Marrara (2015, pp. 513–514).

[117] Saad-Diniz (2018, pp. 32–35).

[118] Marrara (2015, p. 516).

Law No. 12.846/2013 provides for the possibility of entering into leniency agreements with legal entities that effectively collaborate with the investigations (Article 16), producing evidence, swiftly (Paragraph II), that allows the identification of other parties involved in the infraction (Paragraph I). The company must be the first to come forward (Article 16, §1, Paragraph I) and demonstrate its interest in cooperating "*fully and permanently*" (Article 16, §1, Paragraph III), and it is necessary that it has completely ceased its involvement in the infraction (Article 16, §1, Paragraph II).

It should be noted that the agreement will not exempt the legal entity from the obligation to compensate for the damages caused (Article 16, § 3), but it may reduce the penalty by up to 2/3 of the applicable fine (Article 16, § 2). It is important to note the absence of a minimum parameter for the application of the said fine.

Decree No. 8.240/2015, in turn, establishes that leniency agreements will be entered into with legal entities that are involved with harmful acts provided for in the Anti-Corruption Law and in the Procurement Law, provided that information is presented that allows the identification of other parties involved and documents that prove the investigated infraction (Article 28 of Decree No. 8.240/2015).

For the legal entity to be able to enter into the agreement, five requirements are provided for by Article 30:

Article 30

(i) be the first to come forward with the intention of cooperating with the investigations;

(ii) have completely ceased involvement in the harmful act;

(iii) admit its participation in the administrative infraction;

(iv) fully and permanently cooperate with the investigations and be present at all procedural acts to which it is summoned and, finally, as seen previously,

(v) provide information and documents that prove the infraction.

It will be a confidential procedure (Article 31, §1), and if the parties do not, in the end, enter into an agreement, the documents presented will be returned to the proposing legal entity, and the use of them for the purpose of liability will be prohibited (Article 35).

Unlike the competition defence law, in the anti-corruption regulation there is no provision for prior leniency agreements, which discourages the presentation of information in a phase prior to the administrative process.[119]

Despite the fact that the Anti-Corruption Law, with its criticised objective liability, as explained in the Madero conviction, covers the civil and administrative spheres, many studies highlight the penal character that hides behind the substantial sanctions

[119] Marrara (2015, p. 521).

provided for. The penal aspect that can be inferred from reading the norm may be the result of the regulatory context that gave rise to it.

As studied within the framework of anti-corruption regulatory milestones, Law No. 12.846/2013 was the result of a globalised movement and, it can be said, Brazil was late in this respect. In addition to the fact that corruption has historically been addressed and studied in the penal sphere, other countries, influenced by the same international movement, adopted penal norms, which would evidence a possible transitional character of the Brazilian Anti-Corruption Law.[120]

One of the main criticisms made about the business structure in Brazil is the lack of legal certainty for those who choose to enter into an agreement with public bodies. The corporation that decides to negotiate with the State will find itself facing a *multitude* of agencies, a polycentric structure that will culminate in a kind of "*balkanisation of what should by definition present itself as unique*".[121]

The general rule is that negotiations are conducted by the CGU, which, on 20 November 2020, published Execution Protocol No. 1, the purpose of which was to define the procedures for receiving and sharing information and evidence arising from leniency and plea bargain agreements. The document paid special attention to the protocols that must be observed in the case of confidential information. One of the reasons cited for the request for information exchange between state bodies would be to assess the cooperation demonstrated by the legal entity in an ongoing agreement.

The rule thus aimed to strengthen the role of companies as responsible for economic infractions, so that it will be up to them to implement internal controls that are effective in neutralising their risks, considering the reality in which they find themselves.[122] The economic logic significantly influencing decisions made in the realm of collaborative justice is reiterated, especially in a post-Car Wash Brazil.[123]

One of the clauses that appear in leniency agreements concerns the need for the corporation to implement improvements in its *compliance* programme, as the lack of adequacy of internal controls provides an opportunity for deviant behaviour. This means that the agreements entered into generate "*retrospective*" effects, with the compensation for damages caused, and future ones, through the efforts put into practice to avoid recurrence.[124]

Given the evident influence of the American experience, it is interesting to analyse the institutes used there. In addition to *plea-bargaining* agreements, DPAs and NPAs were created there as punitive alternatives to offences committed by minors, first-time defendants and less serious crimes, the initial objective of which was to avoid

---

[120] Salvador Netto (2018, p. 312) and following.

[121] Tojal and Tamasaukas (2020, p. 129).

[122] Salvador Netto (2018, pp. 315–321).

[123] Saad-Diniz (2018, p. 27).

[124] Tojal and Tamasaukas (2020, p. 137).

criminal stigmatisation for young defendants.[125] Their use in agreements with large corporations gained prominence after the 2007/8 crisis.[126]

The agreements initially had three main objectives: (i) to prevent future irregularities; (ii) to save resources of the prosecuting bodies for more important cases; and (iii) to act as a form of obtaining restitution for the communities and victims affected by the irregularity. These scopes would demonstrate that the agreements were originally thought for individuals, especially the second point, showing that the focus would not be on large corporate cases.[127]

In March 2008, the DOJ published the Morford Memorandum,[128] through which it was defined that DPAs would be criminal procedures characterised by the protocol of a charging document by the government, subsequently presented to the judiciary, equating to a procedural suspension, while NPAs would result in no formal charges being brought as a result of an agreement entered into between the parties, without the involvement of the court, whose requirements must be met within a specified period. It is worth remembering that in the *common law* system, the parties have a much more significant role than that observed in *civil law* systems.

As previously studied, the collaboration of companies in investigations has become a criminal political movement of great relevance in the USA and this is due to the logic of efficiency that has also become part of the penal reality: the State, aware of the difficulties it encounters when opting for a trial—in which sufficient evidence must be obtained to allow conviction *beyond reasonable doubt*, plus the time and costs allocated to the whole process—, shifts the duty of cooperation to private agents. These, faced with the threat of high sanctions and the risks (financial and reputational) involved in a trial, will "*choose*" to provide the necessary information for the conclusion of agreements.

On the other hand, DPAs and NPAs can be seen as an alternative for preserving the continuity and financial integrity of companies; Arthur Andersen serves as a negative example of the decision to take a corporation to trial.[129]

Criticisms of this American reality are made in various ways. On one hand, there could be potential abuse of power by prosecutors, in a procedural logic geared towards accusation and the consequent violation of due process, as defendants are asked, albeit subtly, to waive their procedural and fundamental rights (such as professional confidentiality, for example). On the other hand, there are those who question the blatant penal selectivity that allows corporations and their managers to avoid a criminal conviction in exchange for the payment of fines and restructuring plans for internal controls.[130]

---

[125] Reilly (2015, p. 106).

[126] Xiao (2015, p. 234).

[127] Reilly (2015, pp. 108–109).

[128] U.S. Department of Justice. Office of the Deputy Attorney General. *Selection and Use of Monitors in Deferred Prosecution Agreements and Non-Prosecution Agreements with Corporations.* Washington D.C, Mar. 7, 2008.

[129] Xiao (2015, p. 252).

[130] Xiao (2015, pp. 235–236).

At this point, Reilly highlights what would be a fanciful reality—that companies could not withstand criminal indictments, in financial and reputational terms—and questions the role of federal agencies in this narrative.

According to the author, prosecutors would tend to apply the law with a double standard, as the relevance of the company will be decisive in determining whether criminal charges would be brought, considering the possible collateral effects and potential criticisms of the state.[131] The decision (political) to allow the collapse of Lehman Brothers bank can be highlighted as an example that there would be no financial institution too big to fail.

It is also possible to mention the criticism directed at the agreements made in relation to the theory that companies would not withstand criminal charges and, for this reason, would always opt for the path without trial, with the aim of self-preservation. In this vein, Markoff analysed a sample of 54 companies criminally convicted, between the years 2001 and 2010, to verify whether the fear of potential trials would be rational, with the auditing firm Arthur Andersen as a notable case: as an external auditing firm, responsible for validating Enron's accounting information, it was criminally prosecuted for obstructing justice by destroying numerous documents related to the technology company's investigations.[132]

With the loss of its reputational credibility, the aforementioned company faced various financial problems until it ceased to operate. Its closure was attributed, by many, to the confrontation of a complex criminal process, which generated concern that corporations would not be able to face this reality and should, as soon as possible, conclude the procedural instructions through agreements with the state.

Markoff explains, then, that with the strengthening of the respondeat superior theory, the prosecuting bodies saw in legal entities a more effective way to respond to corporate crime, which intensified with the publication of the Sentencing Guidelines and their positive and negative valuations.[133] In his analysis, he found that, contrary to what is widely considered an absolute truth, companies criminally prosecuted do not close their doors after potential convictions.

In his conclusions, Markoff argues that about 90% of trials are concluded by out-of-court settlements, the so-called plea agreements, in which demands for changes and improvements in internal compliance programmes may be included, but that the processes are necessary as a form of deterrence of bad corporate practices.[134]

As an alternative to the policy of entering into DPAs as a first option, the author suggests that agreements be proposed when there is what he classifies as structural harms, that is, structural damages that would put at risk the continuity of service provision and production by the company,[135] returning to its initial purpose of dealing with more relevant cases.

---

[131] Reilly (2015, pp. 114–121).

[132] Markoff (2013, pp. 803–805).

[133] Markoff (2013, p. 803).

[134] Markoff (2013, p. 827) and following.

[135] Markoff (2013, pp. 832–835).

Another criticism presented relates to the theory of respondeat superior, which, although created to deal with compensation for damages in the civil sphere, was strategically transposed to criminal law as a way to ensure convictions of companies for conduct carried out by their representatives.[136]

A recent case of DPA was published on 22.10.2020 by the DOJ, involving the Goldman Sachs Group Inc., based in New York, and Goldman Sachs (Malaysia) Sdn. Bhd. for money laundering and violations of the FCPA, represents the largest agreement signed to date by the American government.[137] The irregularities involve the Malaysian state investment fund 1MDB and the payment of billions of dollars in bribes to secure the financial institution's participation in profitable deals.

According to the DOJ, Goldman Sachs was involved in a broad scheme of international corruption, implemented to the detriment of the Malaysian people and the reputation of American companies, a major concern for the US government, as discussed in the above item related to the FCPA and anti-corruption measures. The 1MDB was supposed to direct investments towards the economic development of Malaysia; however, its funds were used for the payment of bribes that would guarantee commercial advantages for the American financial institution.

As justification for the high financial sanction, the DOJ pointed out the following evaluation criteria: the lack of effective cooperation from Goldman Sachs with the investigations carried out, exemplified by the delay in producing evidence; the severity and nature of the infractions committed, as well as the involvement of the institution's senior management; the involvement of several subsidiaries, considering that the payment of bribes and money laundering involved financial institutions located in other countries, such as Abu Dhabi, and the high amount paid in bribes, exceeding US$1.6 billion.

Finally, it is worth noting that agreements with public bodies can result in the appointment of a monitor who would be assigned, precisely because of the technicality of this figure, internal monitoring functions in relation to the activities performed by the company.

The Morford Memorandum sought to regulate the use of monitors in cases of agreements between the prosecuting bodies and the accused. This is an independent third party who will become part of the corporation with the aim of implementing improvements in the necessary areas, usually in the one involved in the irregularity.

The functions of the monitor tend to vary according to the specific case, but their focus will be to ensure that the agreement made with the public power is fulfilled and, consequently, to prevent recurrence of the offence committed.

The choice, as mentioned, will depend on the characteristics of the case and the agreement made, but three main points should be observed: (i) qualification of the chosen one; (ii) avoid conflicts of interest, existing or potential; and (iii) instilling confidence in the role of the monitor. It should be noted that the monitor should not be seen as a government employee, nor as a company employee, but as an independent

---

136 Reilly (2015, pp. 122) and following.

137 U.S. Department of Justice. *Goldman Sachs Charged in Foreign Bribery Case and Agrees to Pay Over $2.9 Billion.* Oct. 22, 2020.

third party, responsible for evaluating and recommending the efforts implemented by the corporation.

If necessary, the monitor may write reports directed to the government and the company with their comments and evaluations about their performed activities, the progress verified, as well as what is lacking to fulfil the agreement. Direct contact with the government may occur if they become aware of company actions that (i) pose a risk to public health or the environment; (ii) involve the participation of senior management; (iii) practices of obstruction of justice; (iv) criminal practices that can be investigated; or (v) in any situation where there is a chance of causing substantial damage.

If the recommendations made by the monitor are not implemented by the company, it will be up to the public bodies to analyse the given motivation and whether, by not following the provided directions, the company has failed to comply with what was contained in its DPA or NPA. However, if the company can prove that there is no longer a need for the monitor's services, the contract may be terminated early.

In light of this, the figure of the monitor reveals some points that deserve attention. The first would be the competence of the prosecutors in determining changes in organisational cultures and in corporate structures and, once again, the imbalance in the relationship, since it would be up to the government to revoke the agreement and resume the accusatory procedures if it unilaterally understands that the company failed to implement the clauses present in the signed agreement.[138] As widely highlighted in this work, the lack of normative parameters, now on the monitor's performance, brings legal uncertainty for those who have this clause established in their contracts with public bodies.

Although appointed by the State, the monitor will maintain a private contract with the company, which highlights possible conflicts of interest and corporate governance, especially if we consider that, rarely, their functions will be pre-established and also in relation to the flow of information that will exist between the private entity and the State.[139]

In summary, this section sought to bring some discussions about the strengthening of agreements made between companies and the State and the expansion of negotiation techniques in Brazilian Criminal Law, especially in the context of individuals. The American influence on the topic is evident, and caution must be exercised with the "*legal translations*",[140] since foreign institutes tend to implement a chain of changes in the local legal system.

A specific DOJ publication on the choice of monitors was published in October 2018 and became known as the Benczkowski Memorandum. The central point of the document was to ensure the compatibility between the chosen monitor and the technical and specific aspects of the case analysed. Two main points should be considered when choosing a particular monitor, namely: (i) the potential benefits that their

[138] Reilly (2015, pp. 136–146).

[139] Griffin (2011, pp. 119) and following.

[140] Langer (2017, p. 114).

appointment would bring to the company and society and (ii) the costs of this choice and its impacts on business operations.

The Memorandum detailed the selection process of the monitors very much in line with the technicality that was sought with this appointment, in order to ensure its adequacy with the facts and circumstances verified in the specific case. Characteristics such as education, professional experience and relevance, recommendations, and degree of independence were some of the points evaluated in the selection of candidates.

As previously explained, the updated guidance from the Trump administration, in 2025, is that monitors should only be considered when they are truly necessary, which should be analysed in the specific case and after verifying that their appointment will not interfere with the business conducted by the company, nor represent an excessive cost that could not be replaced by the implementation of a better compliance *programme*. Although the need to prove the necessity of the monitor had been determined since 2018, the new guidance seems to aim at reducing, even more effectively, the use of the monitor figure.

It is worth considering the point made by Hassemer regarding criminal negotiation practices, as, in reality, there would not be an effective negotiation, but an exercise of compensation or even balance between the parties, considering what and how much each one, public and private agents, can give up.[141]

3.8 *Due Diligence* and Continuous Risk Monitoring

The dynamism of business activity demands that corporations carry out daily risk monitoring to which they are exposed. In addition to implementing internal analyses that are capable of identifying potential points of concern, they should also evaluate, through so-called *due diligence*, third parties with whom the company is going to do business, whether they are individuals, legal entities, public or private.

Considering that the Anti-Corruption Law expanded the requirements of *know your client*, classic anti-money laundering norms, companies have had to demand from their business partners the same control standards implemented by them internally.

According to Steinberg, "*more things can happen than will happen*" and, in this sense, although risks are part of business, their monitoring can be seen as a way to improve decision-making dynamics, identify opportunities and reduce surprises.[142] It can be said that the model of waiting for the emergence of *red flags* to act represents an outdated and insufficient practice for current regulatory demands. With risk assessment, the company can discover the *etiological factors* of behaviours that threaten its activity.[143]

---

[141] Hassemer (1994, p. 48).

[142] Steinberg (2011, p. 75).

[143] Nieto Martín (2013, p. 29).

These behaviours can be individual or collective.

It is important to note that the implementation of *due diligence* practices and risk monitoring are two distinct aspects of the compliance *programme.* In risk assessment, the company will need to understand the market in which it operates, identifying threats and characteristics that will require greater attention.

From this point, the aim is to evaluate what has been identified with the existing internal structure and answer the following question: are the internal controls sufficient to monitor the company's activities? This answer must be appropriate to the reality that is sought to be implemented in the sense that the company does not become a "*Corporate* Big Brother".

In the risk analysis proposed by the CGU, the company, according to its specificities, should map[144]:

(i) the sectors of the market, Brazilian and foreign, in which it operates;
(ii) the organisational structure, here considering factors such as hierarchy, decision-making processes, and tasks assigned to executive members;
(iii) the size of the company and relations with third parties;
(iv) the level of interaction with public authorities and weight attributed to processes that depend on them (tenders, authorisations, government licenses) and
(v) the shareholdings.

Given this context, risk management will involve two equally important fronts, that is, the definition of processes and policies that can address problems that have already occurred in the company, and the identification of potential events that may, in some way, cause impacts in the future.[145]

In this assessment, the analysis of characteristics such as (i) the company's profile; (ii) the market sector in which it operates; (iii) its organisational structure; (iv) the risks considered inherent; and (v) the integrations carried out with society will be decisive.[146]

To develop a risk map, a correlation must be made between the impact caused and the likelihood of that event actually occurring (probability). This allows determining which variables will be considered when implementing internal controls. Even if less likely, major risks should not be off the companies' radar, whether they are image or financial risks.

Here we can revisit the discussion related to risk-based analysis, mentioned when we discussed policies related to the prevention of money laundering and corrupt practices. By determining their risk appetite, corporations will establish operating parameters and risk limits they are willing to face. After identifying risk situations, specific controls aimed at reducing the possibility of harmful acts occurring will be developed.

---

144 Office of the Comptroller General. *Integrity Programme: Guidelines for Private Companies*, 2015.

145 Steinberg (2011, p. 80).

146 Barbosa and Olivé (2019, p. 25).

One of the main points of attention in developing a compliance programme is not to assume that good internal policies remain positive (and effective) by inertia. As an example, the case of Johnson & Johnson can be cited, which in the 80s discovered a problem with one of its drugs and immediately removed all products from the stores where they were sold. However, when faced with a similar problem in the late 2000s, the company took a different path, ignoring the red flags related to systemic irregularities in its productions, resulting in criminal investigations, financial and reputational losses.[147]

Continuous monitoring of risks and internal controls, carried out through routine reports, monitoring of complaints, and the relationship maintained with regulatory bodies, allows the company to validate its current processes and check which points require action.

The case of Embraer, on the other hand, highlights the importance of conducting due diligence with the organisation's business partners, especially if the negotiations involved significant amounts and the participation of foreign authorities. In the case of the aviation company, a simpler investigation into the histories of the companies through which the improper payments were made could have drawn attention to the fact that they were front companies used solely to legitimise the bribe payments to the facilitators of aircraft sales in the Dominican Republic, India, Saudi Arabia and Mozambique. This failure was highlighted by the SEC, which pointed out in its report that simple research on the companies' administrators would have been enough to trigger Embraer's internal controls.

Thus, a due control test is proposed to be implemented by the company, through a methodology based on the predictability of the crime, to assess the risks to which it is exposed: internal and external criminogenic factors will be valued periodically, to determine which areas of the company tend to require more attention and prevention procedures.[148] Once these risks are mapped, their effectiveness is evaluated through training, management efforts and the coherence identified between the mapped red flags and the internal policies put into effect and, if necessary, implement the necessary changes.[149]

To assess business risks, methodologies such as those published by the Committee of Sponsoring Organizations of the Treadway Commission ("COSO") can be used, aimed at developing controlled environments from the assessment of external and internal risks to the company's activity. From this point, implementation is carried out through three fronts: (i) control activities, with policies and procedures for action; (ii) information and communication; and (iii) supervision, when the adequacy of controls to new risks is verified.[150]

The COSO methodology is a consolidated way to manage the identified corporate risks.

---

[147] Steinberg (2011, pp. 27–29).

[148] Nieto Martín (2019, p. 97).

[149] Nieto Martín (2019, pp. 98–100).

[150] Nieto Martín (2019, p. 52).

It is important to note that risk management serves not only to identify risks that may be negative for the corporation, but also to map those that may favour it in obtaining positive business opportunities.[151] Therefore, it is important that the analyses are carried out by multidisciplinary teams that can map controls and processes necessary to ensure that the corporation's activity is always maintained within the allowed risks.

3.9 Crisis Management

Bad things happen to good companies. In the final phase of our analysis, we will examine how a well-structured *compliance* programme will assist the company and its managers in effectively managing a crisis and enable the necessary changes to be implemented so that the irregularity does not recur. Everything from how communications will be made to the market to the internal remedial measures will be relevant to the construction of a solid corporate culture.

The more an economic activity develops, the more difficult it becomes to have knowledge of and control over all the side effects that may result from its operation. In this vein, Beck asserts that each advance in the technical-scientific field should be accompanied by the learning that is absorbed with this step, explaining that the production of wealth will come along with the social production of risks.[152] Based on this assumption, it is not possible, nor expected, that a company can completely eliminate all the risks inherent to its activity, but that it develops controls that allow their prevention.

Two types of risks that should be considered by internal controls can be highlighted: those that will impact the company from an internal point of view and those that will generate effects for its surroundings.

Often the company may be well organised, in terms of *compliance* and corporate governance, and be surprised by a failure in its internal policies that results in unmapped damages. Saad-Diniz considers that *compliance* programmes are the result of a "*constant state of change*" and, therefore, occasional failures should not cause panic, but rather lead to the quick recognition of the need to use them for the implementation of improvements. For the author, more than focusing on punishment, the company needs to continue acting in pursuit of the development of a *pro-social behaviour* and in the *creation of conditions for the exercise of business freedom.*[153]

As mentioned earlier, the discovery of weaknesses in internal procedures represents opportunities to improve *compliance* policies. Nieto Martin emphasises that dealing with the risks of a business activity is equivalent to a *blend* of criminology,

---

[151] Steinberg (2011, p. 85).

[152] Beck (2011, p. 23).

[153] Saad-Diniz (2019, pp. 191–194).

auditing knowledge and procedures, and business *management*.[154] The strengthening of criminological research aimed at mapping the causes and effects of business behaviour in Brazil and the foundations for the development of corporate restorative justice is highlighted.[155]

As verified in the previous items, the existence of improper conduct in the organisation will open a delicate range of decisions that will be determinant for business recovery. We have discussed the importance of ensuring constant flows of information, internal conduct policies properly explained and reinforced by leaders, through internal investigations that will ensure the company's control of information in a complex context of negotiations with public authorities, to periodic risk monitoring. Finally, an effective *compliance* programme will bring the procedures and principles that need to be observed by the company with the aim of repairing the damages caused internally and externally.

After moments of crisis, the company must communicate to the public the facts and measures taken, so it is essential that there is interdisciplinary participation from *marketing* and communication areas to address the problem and the implemented modifications in the best way. It can be seen how clear and transparent language is necessary throughout the development of *compliance* programmes, whether the measures are aimed at its employees or other *stakeholders*.

References

Baldan ÉL (2019) Lineamentos da investigação criminal defensiva no provimento 188/2018 do Conselho Federal da OAB. Boletim IBCCRIM, São Paulo 27(322):7–9

Barbosa PAR, Olivé JCF (2019) Compliance, Derecho Penal Corporativo y Buena Gobernanza Empresarial. Tirant lo Blanch, Bogotá

Beck U (2011) *Sociedade de risco:* rumo a uma outra modernidade, 2nd ed. Editora 34, São Paulo

Chen H, Soltes E (2018) Why compliance programs fail and how to fix them. Available at: https://hbr.org/2018/03/why-compliance-programs-fail. Accessed on 11 Nov 2025

Controladoria-Geral Da UNIÃO (2015) Programa de Integridade: Diretrizes para Empresas Privadas

Costa HRL, Araújo, MPC (2014) Compliance e o julgamento da APn 470. Revista Brasileira de Ciências Criminais 106: 215–230

Dezem GM, Souza LA (2020) Comentários ao Pacote Anticrime: Lei 13.964/2019. Revista dos Tribunais, São Paulo

Dunst LG, Chirlin DJ (2009) A Renewed Emphasis on Upjohn Warnings. Andrews Lit R 23(12)

Estellita H (2015) Quando o crime se oculta na empresa. Folha de São Paulo, November 1

Fairfax RA Jr (2010) Outsourcing criminal prosecution? The limits of criminal justice privatization. Univ Chic Leg Forum 10:266–282

Feldens L, Diettrich EDR (2016) A privatização da função investigatória nos delitos empresariais. In: Feldens L, Estellita H, Wunderlich A (Orgs). Direito Penal Econômico e Empresarial: Estudos dos grupos de pesquisa em Direito Penal Econômico e Empresarial da PUCRS

Ferreira RCA, Okada TSU (2020) Compliance na indústria da moda: corrupção e o caso Ralph Lauren. In: Souza LA (coord) Compliance no Direito Penal. Revista dos Tribunais, São Paulo

[154] Nieto Martín (2013, p. 30).

[155] Saad-Diniz (2019), *passim*.

Franco I (2020) Investigações internas corporativas em todos os tempos. In: Carvalhosa M, Kuyven F (coords) Compliance no Direito Empresarial. Revista dos Tribunais, São Paulo
Friedman M (1970) The social responsibility of business is to increase its profits. The New York Times, Sep. 13
García-Moreno B (2020) *Del whistleblower al alertador:* la regulación europea de los canales de denúncia. Tirant Lo Blanch, Valencia
Griffin LK (2011) Inside-out enforcement. In: Barkow RE, Barkon AS (eds) Prosecutors in the Boardroom: using criminal law to regulate corporate conduct. New York University Press, New York
Hassemer W (1994) Perspectivas de uma moderna política criminal. Revista Brasileira de Ciências Criminais, São Paulo, 2(8):41–51
Langer M (2017) Dos Transplantes Jurídicos às traduções jurídicas: a globalização pelo *plea bargaining* e a tese da americanização do processo penal. Delictae 2(3), July/Dec
Laufer WS (2002) Corporate prosecution, cooperation and the trading of favors. Iowa L Rev 87(2), Jan
Markoff G (2013) Arthur Andersen and the myth of the corporate death penalty: corporate criminal convictions in the twenty-first century. Univ Pennsylvania J Bus L 15:643–667
Maroto Calatayud M (2008) Liberalismo vs. neocorporativismo: los discursos de la autorregulación como discursos legitimantes. In: Arroyo Jiménez L, Nieto Martín A (dirs) Autorregulación y sanciones. Lex Nova, Valladolid
Marrara T (2015) Acordos de leniência no processo administrativo brasileiro: modalidades, regime jurídico e problemas emergentes. Revista Digital de Direito Administrativo 2(2):509–527
Martin SL (2015) Compliance officers: more jobs, more responsibility, more liability. Notre Dame J L Ethics Pub Pol 29, pp 169–198
Matos EDA (2018) Colaboração premiada: análise de sua utilização na Operação Lava Jato à luz da verossimilhança e da presunção de inocência. Revista Brasileira de Ciências Criminais, São Paulo, p 143
Montiel JP (2013) Sentido y alcance de las investigaciones internas en la empresa. Revista de Derecho de la Pontifícia Universidad Católica de Valparaíso XL
Moosmayer K (2013) Investigaciones internas: una introducción a sus problemas esenciales. In: Arroyo Zapatero L, Nieto Martín A (dirs) El Derecho Penal Económico en la era Compliance. Tirant Lo Blanch, Valencia
Near JP, Miceli MP (1985) Organizational dissidence: the case of whistle-blowing. J Bus Ethics 4(1):1–16
Nieto Martín A (2012) Cosmetic use and lack of precision in compliance programs: any solution?
Nieto Martín A (2013) Problemas fundamentales del cumplimiento normativo en el derecho penal. In: Kuhlen L, Montiel JP, Ortiz de Urbina Gimeno Í (eds) Compliance y teoria del derecho penal. Marcial Pons, Madrid
Nieto Martín A (2019a) Compliance, Criminologia e Responsabilidade penal da pessoa jurídica. In: Nieto Martín A et al (orgs) Manual de cumprimento normativo e responsabilidade penal das pessoas jurídicas. 2nd ed. Tirant Lo Blanch, São Paulo, pp 62–122
Nieto Martín A (2019b) Código de Ética, avaliação de riscos, educação e treinamento. In: Nieto Martín A et al. (orgs) Manual de cumprimento normativo e responsabilidade penal das pessoas jurídicas. 2nd ed. Tirant Lo Blanch, São Paulo, pp 163–190
Nieto Martín A (2019c) Internal investigations. In: Nieto Martín A et al (orgs) Manual de cumprimento normativo e responsabilidade penal das pessoas jurídicas. 2nd ed. Tirant Lo Blanch, São Paulo, pp 293–334
Nieto Martín A (2019d) Fundamento e Estrutura dos Programas de Compliance. In: Nieto Martín A et al (orgs) Manual de cumprimento normativo e responsabilidade penal das pessoas jurídicas. 2nd ed. Tirant Lo Blanch, São Paulo, pp 131–154
OECD (2013) Anti-corruption ethics and compliance handbook for business
Office of the Comptroller General (2015) Integrity programme: guidelines for private companies

Paine LS (1994) Managing for organizational integrity. Available at: https://hbr.org/1994/03/managing-for-organizational-integrity
Pinto NR (2017) A importância dos marcos regulatórios na prevenção à criminalidade econômica. LiberArs, São Paulo
Ramm A (2018) It's the end of Privilege as we know it and I (don't) feel fine: the deterioration of the corporate attorney-client privilege and work product protection in the European Union, United Kingdom and Germany. Univ Cincin L Rev, 87:301–323
Ragués i Vallès R (2006) ¿Héroes o traidores? La protección de los informantes internos (whistleblowers) como estrategia político-criminal. InDret pp 1–19
Ragués i Vallès R (2013) Whistleblowing: una aproximación desde el derecho penal. Editora Marcial Pons, Madrid
Reilly PR (2014) Ralph Lauren, Transnational Bribery and Voluntary Disclosure under the Foreign Corrupt Practices Act: when is it strategically wise (or not) to self-report FCPA violations to the SEC? Harvard Bus L Rev. Available at: https://clsbluesky.law.columbia.edu/2014/03/03/ralph-lauren-transnational-briberyand-voluntary-disclosure-under-the-foreign-corrupt-practices-act-when-is-it-strategically-wise-or-not-to-self-reportfcpa-violations-to-the-sec/
Reilly PR (2015) Justice Deferred is Justice Denied: we must end our failed experiment in Deferring Corporate Criminal Prosecutions. Brigham Young Univ L Rev, 307–358
Rodrigues AM (2018) Compliance programs and corporate criminal compliance. Revista Brasileira de Ciências Criminais, São Paulo 26(149):17–28
Rodríguez VG, Saad-Diniz E, Marin, GDC (2020) Programas de whistleblowing e os problemas da delação premiada. In: Souza, Luciano Anderson de (Coord.) Compliance no Direito Penal. Revista dos Tribunais, São Paulo
Saad-Diniz E (2018) Brasil v. Golias: os 30 anos da responsabilidade penal da pessoa jurídica e as novas tendências em compliance. Revista dos Tribunais 107(988):25–53
Saad-Diniz E (2019) *Ética negocial e compliance:* entre a educação executiva e a interpretação judicial. Thomson Reuters Brasil, São Paulo
Salvador Netto AV (2018) Responsabilidade Penal da Pessoa Jurídica. Revista dos Tribunais, São Paulo
Silva Sánchez JM (2004) Eficiência e Direito Penal. Manole, Barueri
Silveira RDMJ (2014) O Acordo de Leniência na Lei Anticorrupção. Revista dos Tribunais 947:157–177
Silveira RDMJ, Saad-Diniz E (2015) Compliance, Direito Penal e Lei Anticorrupção. Saraiva, São Paulo
Silveira RDMJ (2020) Direito Penal da era compliance, a realidade penal econômico-empresarial brasileira e a variação de seus momentos. In: Souza LA (coord) Compliance no Direito Penal. Revista dos Tribunais, São Paulo
Souza ABG (2020) O informante no contexto dos sistemas de compliance. In: Barboza MN, Walmsley A, Cireno L (orgs) Inovações da Lei nº 13.964, de 24 de dezembro de 2019. 2a Câmara de Coordenação e Revisão do MPF, Brasília
Steinberg RM (2011) Governance, risk management and compliance: it can't happen to us—avoiding corporate disaster while driving success. Wiley, Hoboken, NJ
Steinberg RM (2012) The game changes: 10 essential elements for truly effective compliance programs
Stevens B (1994) An analysis of corporate ethical code studies: "Where do we go from here?" J Bus Ethics 13, 63–69
Sutherland EH (2015) White Collar crime: uncut version, 1st edn. Revan Publishing, Rio de Janeiro
Teixeira A, Wehrs C (2020) Proteção do Sigilo de Comunicação entre Advogado e Empresa em Investigações Internas: Os Casos Jones Day E SFO V. ENRC. Instituto de Cooperação Jurídica Internacional—newsletter, 05 abr. 2019
Tojal SBB, Tamasauskas IS (2020) Decifrando a esfinge: como o sistema de multiplicidade institucional anticorrupção brasileiro permitiu que se produzissem meia centena de acordos de

leniência. In: Carvalhosa M, Kuyven F (coords) Compliance no Direito Empresarial. Revista dos Tribunais, São Paulo
U.S. Department of Justice (2003) Office of the Deputy Attorney General. Principles of Federal Prosecution of Business Organizations, Jan
U.S. Department of Justice (2008) Office of the Deputy Attorney General. Selection and Use of Monitors in Deferred Prosecution Agreements and Non-Prosecution Agreements with Corporations. Washington D.C., Mar 7
U.S. Department of Justice (2015) Office of the Deputy Attorney General. Individual accountability for corporate wrongdoing, Sep
U.S. Department of Justice (2020) Goldman Sachs charged in foreign bribery case and agrees to pay over $2.9 billion, Oct 22
Wellner PA (2005) Effective compliance programs and corporate criminal prosecutions. Cardozo L Rev 27(1):497–528
Xiao MY (2015) Deferred/non prosecution agreements: effective tools to combat corporate crime. Cornell J L Pub Pol 23, 497–528
Zilli M (2017) No acordo de colaboração entre gregos e troianos o cavalo é o prêmio. Boletim IBCCRIM, São Paulo, n.300, Nov

Chapter 4
Final Considerations

The need for adherence to *compliance* programmes has been driven by Anglo-Saxon pressure to avoid corruption and money laundering crimes on an international scale. In this context, the 1977 *Foreign Corrupt Practices Act* (FCPA) is noteworthy, aiming to hold American individuals and entities civilly and criminally liable for corrupt practices involving public officials, state authorities, and politicians from foreign countries, among other things, obstructing competition.

Furthermore, signalling the international movement to prevent companies from gaining advantages through corrupt acts at the expense of honest companies, the UK's anti-bribery legislation, the UK *Bribery Act* 2010 (UKBA), stands out. Considered pioneering, it was responsible for introducing criminal liability for collective entities and the criminalisation of private corruption.

In the Brazilian context, it is noted that the Anti-Corruption Law (Law No. 12.846/2013), although not in great depth, was the first national regulation to define *compliance* programmes, establishing in Article 7, Clause VIII, as a circumstance to be considered in the application of sanctions:

> the existence of mechanisms and internal procedures for integrity, auditing and encouragement to report irregularities and the effective application of codes of ethics and conduct within the legal entity.

The Money Laundering Law (Law No. 9.613/1998), in turn, established the duty of *compliance* for obligated persons (Article 10, Clause III). The persons referred to in Article 9, in turn, must adopt policies, procedures and internal controls, compatible with their size and volume of operations. The obligation, however, does not refer to the creation of mechanisms to prevent the commission of laundering, but aims to

---

Supplementary Information The online version contains supplementary material available at https://doi.org/10.1007/978-3-032-15011-0_4.

L. A. d. Souza and N. R. Pinto, *Criminal Compliance – Concepts and Implementation*,
https://doi.org/10.1007/978-3-032-15011-0_4

create policies, procedures and internal controls to maintain records of information and notifications of suspicious activities.

The New Procurement Law, finally, provides in Article 25, Paragraph 4, for the implementation of compliance programmes by the winning company of the bidding process, in the following terms:

> In contracts for large-scale works, services and supplies, the tender document must provide for the obligation to implement an integrity programme by the winning bidder, within 6 (six) months, counted from the signing of the contract, according to regulations that will provide for the measures to be adopted, the form of proof and the penalties for non-compliance.

In a general context, scandals in the realm of economic crime have fostered the development and enhancement by companies and legislators of new vectors such as "*compliance programmes*", "*risk management*", "*corporate governance*", "*business ethics*", "*codes of conduct*", "*corporate social responsibility*" and, more recently, "*environmental, social and corporate governance*" (*ESG - Environmental, social and corporate governance*).

The adoption of a *compliance* programme represents the incorporation of suitable and effective preventive measures within the business organisation, constituting an appropriate tool to minimise the risks of criminal liability of the company (in cases of environmental crimes, in Brazil) or administrative, as well as criminal or administrative, of its employees and members in management positions.

Naturally, the creation and maintenance of such programmes, despite potentially slowing down market dynamics, as they control more aggressive business postures by mitigating risks, introduces the element of *trust* in relationships, as following governance guidelines reduces the margin of criminal liability and enhances corporate reputation.

In addition to positive effects such as adding value, serving as a competitive advantage, influencing the positive perception of *stakeholders* such as investors, customers, governments, and competitors, the programme serves as an indication of the absence of intent, noting that it does not exclude liability for negligence in cases provided for by law—which, it should be noted, is not the case for corruption or money laundering, given the absence of provision for the negligent modality.

For *criminal compliance* to constitute a tool for preventing corporate crime, it must be effective and not just a speculative manoeuvre or business *marketing* strategy to deceive the market and control bodies. Indeed, there is a danger in creating vague compliance mechanisms that open the door to indiscriminate assignment of responsibility.

In this regard, in addition to the code of conduct and internal policies, it is necessary to implement a system of training and internalisation of the crime prevention model, forming part of the corporate culture itself, requiring constant review that detects new ways of committing offences.

The *criminal compliance*, like any other certification, does not automatically function as a "*papal bull*" ensuring judicial acquittal of any offence committed in the company, considering that the criminal process is governed by the free evaluation of evidence,[1] but the creation of compliance programmes, with codes of conduct, whistleblowing channels and monitoring, can serve as mitigation of the penalty or even non-application of penalty, depending on the situation, as well as a form of defence. It is, in short, an important mechanism for risk avoidance and mitigation, or exclusion, of liabilities.

In criminological-political terms, speaking of globalisation as a challenge to Criminal Law is no longer a novelty. For some time now, what was understood as the *ultima ratio* of the State has come to be seen as a regulatory strategy aimed at ensuring feelings such as trust and the smooth functioning of markets. The dynamism and complexity of economic activities demand from Criminal Law a speed alien to its structures and insist on the logic that punitivism would be the solution to all problems.

Throughout this presentation, it was possible to verify how regulation seems to always be late to the party, trying to prevent situations that have already happened and avoid practices that have already been surpassed. If we think about the financial sphere, for example, the dynamics of the "*cat and mouse*" game become even clearer. Major financial scandals demand from Criminal Law a preventive action to avoid the negative outcomes experienced from repeating in the future.

In this context, the aim is to regain the trust of market participants through the publication of increasingly rigorous and open criminal norms, requiring a multidisciplinary analysis to know exactly what the prohibited conduct is. The result, as always, is symbolic.

In recent years, we have daily witnessed the result of major criminal operations that highlighted the lack of internal organisation of multinationals that represented the entire strength of the capitalist system, and we saw compliance programmes being elevated to the category of solution to all problems.

Nieto Martín categorises four types of existing regulation, in his conception, that would result in the development of *compliance* programmes, as a state tool for creating market balance and transparency among companies:

(i) a very detailed and uniform regulation to all markets, which, for the author, would lead to irrational and inefficient situations;
(ii) the so-called *creative compliance*, characterised by symbolic compliance with the norm, since the applicable norms are seen as bureaucratic and excessively costly;
(iii) the *regulatory capture*, developed from contact with market participants, often the result of *lobbying* and influences from major *players* and, the fourth model would be the
(iv) police model, in which the focus tends to be on sanctioning rather than promoting compliance policies.[2]

---

[1] González Franco and Blumenberg (2013, p. 158).

[2] Nieto Martín (2019, p. 37).

Reading many texts reveals that current *compliance* programmes seem to be a mix of what would be least effective in the four proposed models. Companies tend to implement minimum controls that meet more the expectations of the regulator than internal needs, resulting in symbolic programmes, which can also be seen as a result of the lack of normative prediction about what will be considered effective by the *enforcement* agencies.

In this research, it was possible to highlight that, more than being a mirror to the failed expansions of Criminal Law, integrity programmes should primarily focus on the development of good corporate cultures and the concern with integrating *compliance* into internal decisions.

Anabela Rodrigues establishes an evaluation of *compliance* programmes based on a test composed of two metrics, the first being *abstract* and the second *practical*[3]. In the first case, one should verify the effectiveness of the programme through the more formal aspects such as, for example, answering questions like "*did the company offer training?*", "*was the whistleblowing channel known and used by employees?*", "*did the code of conduct foresee situations faced by the company and was it complied with?*", while the concrete test would be related to the existence of internal controls aimed at the problem that occurred, in order to identify what could have failed and given space to the irregularity.

If the first point would seek to identify possible failures in the development of the *compliance* programme, the second would analyse the failures in the project implementation. What we propose in this paper is that these questions be answered within the reality of the company, always keeping in mind that formalism will not represent, in the long term, an improvement in the business environment.

The values of the *compliance* programmes should be clear to corporate leaders and all workers linked to the company, and should not be merely various tools and controls implemented with the sole objective of proving, to *enforcement* bodies, a symbolic compliance with the norm.

References

González Franco JA, Schemmel A, Blumenberg A (2013). La función del penalista en la confección, implementación y evaluación de los programas de cumplimento. In: Arroyo Zapatero L, Nieto Martín A (Orgs), El derecho penal económico en la era compliance, Tirant lo Blanch, Valencia

Nieto Martín A (2019) O cumprimento normativo. In: Nieto Martín A et al. (Orgs.), Manual de cumprimento normativo e responsabilidade penal das pessoas jurídicas. 2nd ed. Tirant Lo Blanch, São Paulo, pp 29–53

Rodrigues AM (2018) Compliance programs and corporate criminal compliance. Revista Brasileira de Ciências Criminais 26(149):17–28

[3] Rodrigues (2018, p. 22).

Chapter 5
Collection of Cases

The analysis of some paradigmatic cases proves to be an important tool for the achievement of effective *compliance* programmes, as well as revealing how the authorities viewed the situations, which allows for better corporate planning. The hypotheses referenced were pointed out throughout this work.

5.1 Morgan Stanley and Garth Peterson Case

The case involving Morgan Stanley & Co., Inc.'s ("*Morgan Stanley*") and one of its directors, Garth Peterson, responsible for real estate investments in China, exemplifies the importance of having internal controls and company organisation to prove the implemented efforts and that the actions of one of its agents were, in fact, a one-off irregularity.

The irregularities investigated by the regulatory bodies, DOJ and SEC, were carried out between the years 2002 and 2008 ("*period analyzed*"), when Peterson was acting as an agent of the financial institution in Asia.

As demonstrated in the case files, Morgan Stanley proved that it maintained a *compliance* programme specifically aimed at the *Foreign Corrupt Practices Act* ("*FCPA*"), with constant training and heightened attention to payment control, especially with regard to transfers made to public agents. It had about 500 *compliance officers* in its organisations dedicated entirely to the development and implementation of improvements in their internal policies and procedures which involved, among other practices, face-to-face and *online* training, *hotlines* prepared to receive information in various languages, including Chinese, and a highlight was reminders sent to its employees, with the good practices provided for in the internal policies related to the FCPA.

During the analysed period, 54 trainings were conducted for the employees located in the Asian continent. Among them, Peterson received at least 7 trainings, in addition

L. A. d. Souza and N. R. Pinto, *Criminal Compliance – Concepts and Implementation*,
https://doi.org/10.1007/978-3-032-15011-0_5

to reminders related to the FCPA. Among his duties, Peterson had the duty to evaluate, negotiate, acquire, and manage the real estate investments made by Morgan Stanley, which is why he had a fiduciary duty to the clients.[1]

The irregularities committed by Peterson involved fraud and false accounting statements provided to the company and involved the participation of a Chinese government official and a Canadian lawyer, both friends of the director and partners in the company *Asiasphere Holdings Limited* ("*Asiasphere*"), based in the British Virgin Islands. This company was presented to the financial institution, during the *due diligences* carried out as an *offshore,* through which the Chinese state-owned company Shanghai Yongye Enterprise ("*Yongye*"), responsible for the development of the Luwan District in Shanghai, would operate. The Chinese official, involved in the irregularities, acted as president of Yongye, exercising control of the company and having authority to make decisions on its behalf.

Through Yongye, which became a major partner in Morgan Stanley's real estate investments in China, the accused aimed to acquire stakes in the financial institution's funds in the businesses carried out in the so-called "*Project* Cavity". The strategy was for Peterson to participate on both sides of the negotiation, since Yongye was actually controlled by the three accused. In *emails* exchanged with other representatives of Morgan Stanley, Peterson made a point of highlighting the important participation of the Chinese official in the negotiations carried out in Asia, even stating that there was a debt with him ("*everyone pls keep in mind the big Picture here. YY* [Yongye] *gave us this deal...So we owe them a favour relating to this deal*").

Add to this the fact that Peterson at no time revealed his shareholding in Asiasphere or in other businesses carried out with the Chinese official, although one of the *compliance* policies of Morgan Stanley requested the immediate disclosure of this type of information. When accused of practices related to corruption in China, through front companies that negotiated with Morgan Stanley, Peterson pleaded guilty.

In addition to dismissal, as a penalty, Peterson was sentenced to restitution. The total amount of US$3,822,613.44 was imposed, and he was also prohibited from working in the securities market. He was further sentenced to 9 months in prison by the DOJ.

Regarding the legal entity, the DOJ publication provides the following justification for the financial institution not being prosecuted:

> After considering all the available facts and circumstances, including that Morgan Stanley constructed and maintained a system of internal controls, which provided reasonable assurances that its employees were not bribing government officials, the Department of Justice declined to bring any enforcement action against Morgan Stanley related to Peterson's conduct. The company voluntarily disclosed this matter and has cooperated throughout the department's investigation.[2]

---

[1] Securities and Exchange Commission. SEC v. Garth Ronald Peterson, no. 12-cv-2033 (E.D.N.Y. 2012).

[2] U.S. Department of Justice. *Former Morgan Stanley Managing Director Pleads Guilty for Role in Evading Internal Controls Required by FCPA*. 25 April 2012".

The SEC shared the same view, publishing the following information:

> Morgan Stanley, which is not charged in the matter, cooperated with the SEC's inquiry and conducted a thorough internal investigation to determine the scope of the improper payments and other misconduct involved.[3]

It can be seen that Morgan Stanley was able to prove that it had a robust compliance programme in place, as well as internal controls that allowed the irregularity to be mapped, and proved that Peterson had received appropriate training but chose to act contrary to the corporation's existing policies.[4] In this regard, the existence of documents demonstrating the diligent performance of the financial institution was of utmost importance, showing that the director's irregular conduct was a one-off failure.

5.2 HSBC Case

In an agreement reached with the DOJ in 2012,[5] the financial institutions HSBC Holdings and HSBC Bank USA N.A. (collectively "*HSBC*") agreed to pay US$1.256 billion due to failures in their internal controls related to money laundering prevention. These deficiencies were characterised by the US Department of Justice as "stunning failures of oversight", as they allowed bank customers to launder at least US$881 million, customers linked to drug trafficking and countries that required greater scrutiny in the analysis of transactions carried out through the financial institution (examples include Cuba, Iran, Libya, and Sudan).

The investigations showed that, between 2006 and 2010, especially the HSBC based in Mexico failed to implement internal controls capable of adequately monitoring the suspicious transactions it intermediated.[6] The problem was widespread in the financial conglomerate with the fact that, despite all the evidence, the Mexican HSBC was internally categorised as standard risk.

It was also found that the clients involved with drug trafficking were linked to the Black Market Peso Exchange (BMPE), a complex illegal system developed to facilitate the sending of illicit money from US cartels abroad, especially to Colombia. In addition to not monitoring transactions, the bank removed relevant information from transactions that allowed it to be verified that they originated from or were destined for high-risk money-laundering countries.

---

[3] Securities and Exchange Commission. *SEC charges former Morgan Stanley executive with FCPA violations and investment adviser fraud*. 25 April 2012: "*Morgan Stanley, which was not convicted for these facts, cooperated with the SEC's investigations and conducted a thorough internal investigation to determine the scope of the improper payments and other irregularities involved.*" (free translation).

[4] Steinberg (2012, pp. 3–4).

[5] U.S. Department of Justice. *HSBC Holdings Plc. and HSBC Bank USA N.A. Admit to Anti-Money Laundering and Sanctions Violations, Forfeit $1.256 Billion in Deferred Prosecution Agreement.* 11 December 2012.

[6] Barbosa and Olivé (2019, p. 32).

According to the prosecutors in charge of the case, the fine imposed was significant due to HSBC's insufficient controls and had the promotional character that no company would be exempt from being held accountable for its mistakes, regardless of its size (concern with the theory of too big to fail). In addition to paying the fine, HSBC committed to improving its internal anti-money laundering policies and implementing an effective compliance programme for its needs, even suspending bonus payments to its highest-ranking executives for a period of five years.

Although the public prosecutor of the State of New York stated that the US financial system would not be used as a vehicle by international criminals, the signing of the Deferred Prosecution Agreement ("DPA") with HSBC was heavily criticised. The press, at the time, highlighted that the hefty fine imposed on the economic group was, in reality, the bank's income in five weeks. According to a report by Rolling Stone, the envelopes used by the cartels to deposit money in HSBC, "would make Tony Montana's travel bags envious", in the film Scarface.[7]

In the words of the Attorney General, Lanny Breuer[8]:

> From 2006 to 2010, the Sinaloa Cartel in Mexico, the Norte del Valle Cartel in Colombia, and other drug traffickers laundered at least $881m in illegal narcotics trafficking proceeds through HSBC Bank USA. These traffickers didn't have to try very hard. They would sometimes deposit hundreds of thousands of dollars in cash, in a single day, into a single account, using boxes designed to fit the precise dimensions of the teller windows in HSBC Mexico's branches.
>
> The justification given by the prosecutors for not individually indicting HSBC's executives was also questioned. The expressed concern that criminal liability of executives could harm the stability of the financial system, causing serious side effects, and the proposal to defer the payment of the executives' bonuses, as an example of improvements in corporate governance, were not well received by the press, considering that such measures would highlight the state's differential treatment of white-collar criminals in relation to the procedural procedures applied to other drug-related crimes (*double standard*).

5.3 Volkswagen Case

In a nutshell, the allegation of fraud involving the Volkswagen Group ("*VW*"), in the USA, is related to the violation of the *Clean Air Act,* considering the use of technologies that aimed to manipulate the results of tests conducted to measure the amount of pollutants emitted by vehicles sold in the USA, as well as the false statements presented for the importation of goods.[9]

The scandal, which became known as *Dieselgate*, involved irregularities committed by VW in the period between 2006 and 2015, when electronic devices were produced with the intention of deceiving US regulators and consumers. The purpose of the *Clean Air Act* is to implement regulations that seek to protect human health and

---

[7] Taibbi (2012).

[8] Peston (2012).

[9] Barbosa and Olivé (2019, p. 41).

the environment, among other ways, by reducing pollutants emitted by motor vehicles. Thus, the *Environmental Protection Agency* ("*EPA*") established standards and procedures for testing the emission of pollutants in vehicles, issuing a certificate for those suppliers approved in the tests. Without this certificate, cars cannot be sold in the USA.

To obtain certification, companies needed to submit a request to the EPA for each model and vehicle group they intended to sell in the North American market. The request, delivered in writing, should be signed by a company representative and contain, among other information, the test results, a description of the engine, and the developed emission controls, including a detailing of each auxiliary device used to control the emission of pollutants.

It is noteworthy that California, through the *California Air Resources Board* ("*CARB*"), has its own certification of approval for vehicles sold in the state, called an *executive order.* To comply with both regulations, VW would need to develop an onboard system capable of monitoring all systems and components related to pollutant emissions.

In mid-2006, VW began to develop a new 2.0 diesel engine model, seen as a milestone for the company's future projects. However, the supervisors realised that they would not be able to develop an engine that complied with the requirements of the regulatory authorities and that, at the same time, was attractive to US consumers. The solution found was the development of a *software* that could circumvent the requirements of the mandatory tests.

Considering that the test procedures were public, VW managed to implement in the system the necessary characteristics to achieve the expected results: the *software* could identify when it was being tested and when the vehicle was running under normal conditions. In the latter situation, the vehicles would emit 35 times more pollutants.

In 2012, VW engineers suspected that some hardware problems presented by the vehicles could be related to the existence of the *software* fraudster, but were encouraged, by company executives, to implement improvements exactly in the *strategy,* that is, in the *software* that would allow them to deceive the tests of the authorities in the USA. The update of the internal controls was applied to all VW vehicles.

Discovered by chance by an institute conducting studies on the possibility of diesel being considered a clean fuel, the *International Council for Clean Transportation* ("*ICCT*"), the fraud was reported to the regulatory bodies in 2014, when it was realised that, in fact, VW cars emitted pollutants at much higher levels than those reported and, especially, allowed. Even so, when questioned, the VW representatives provided detailed responses indicating that the identified issues were mechanical, masking the real origin of pollutant emissions.

The fraud cost the German company $4.3 billion in criminal, civil, environmental, and customs fines.[10] Furthermore, the company committed to fully cooperate with the

---

[10] U.S. Department of Justice. Volkswagen AG Agrees to Plead Guilty and Pay $4.3 Billion in Criminal and Civil Penalties; Six Volkswagen Executives and Employees are Indicted in Connection with Conspiracy to Cheat U.S. Emissions Tests. Jan.11/2017.

investigations, which would involve handing over any and all documents requested by government authorities, the necessary implementation of improvements to its *compliance* programme, and the appointment of an independent monitor who would oversee the company's activities for a period of three years.

For the selection of the monitor, the company could select a shortlist of three candidates, with the state appointing the winner, who should possess the following characteristics: (i) *expertise* in relation to federal anti-fraud regulations; (ii) experience in the development and review of *compliance* programmes, internal controls, as well as ethics and integrity policies; (iii) knowledge about the automotive industry or similar; (iv) ability to access and utilise resources from the evaluated companies, when necessary; and (v) sufficient independence to perform their functions.

The monitor's duties would involve addressing and reducing the risk of recurrence of the irregularities committed by VW and assessing the commitment of the Board members and the company's administrators to internal regulations. Given the limited time available, it was not expected that the monitor would have access to all company information, which is why their activities were planned considering the *risk-based approach* methodology. The monitor would be responsible for producing updated reports on the company, with recommendations for necessary improvements to internal controls. The company would have the duty to assimilate the proposals presented and, if they disagreed with them, to provide justifications proving the lack of necessity.

The negative points that influenced the dosimetry of the penalty applied to VW involved the severity of the irregularity committed by the company, the proven intention to defraud the tests carried out, obstruction of justice by destroying documents related to the fraud, the fact that it did not voluntarily report the improper practices to the US government, and the *marketing* carried out by VW about the cleanliness of the diesel emitted into the atmosphere by its vehicles. As a favourable point, the company's positive history was considered. Six executives were also charged with the fraud perpetrated in the US market. It is estimated that the technology was installed in approximately 600,000 vehicles sold in the US between 2009 and 2014.

As part of the agreement signed by the company, VW committed to ensuring that those responsible for carrying out emission tests would no longer be part of the same team as the system developers. Furthermore, VW would test all its vehicles, including those powered by petrol, as well as create a channel for *whistleblowers* and surveys among employees, which would involve the participation and evaluation of independent auditors.

5.4 Embraer Case

The case involving Embraer S.A. serves as a good example to be discussed in this work due to some of its characteristics. It is a case where the internal investigation was initiated in Brazil by the company after notification by the SEC in 2010 and relates to accusations of bribery of public officials in the Dominican Republic, Saudi

Arabia, India, and Mozambique with the aim of assisting the company in closing aircraft sales contracts in 2007, 2008, and 2010. According to the accusations, undue advantages were paid to public officials, which were generally transferred through consultancy contracts and as sales commissions paid to third-party companies.[11]

In the case of the Dominican Republic, for example, the purchase of two aircraft, at an approximate value of $96.4 million, had to be approved by the Dominican Senate and, in this context, the public official, a colonel in the Armed Forces, would have acted as a facilitator of the negotiations, presenting the aircraft and advocating the contract's closure as an advantage to the country. In exchange, the colonel would receive about 3.7% of the sales value, which would be recorded in the company's balance sheets as sales commissions in commercial expense accounts, a method found by Embraer's agents to circumvent the company's internal controls that did not allow the payment of representation contracts after the business was conducted. The exchange of *emails*, used as evidence by the CVM in the accusation of two administrators, showed the public official's insistence that the *agreement* be maintained after the purchase of the aircraft by the Dominican Republic.

The same conduct was identified in dealings with public officials in Saudi Arabia and Mozambique, where high-ranking members of their respective governments influenced the negotiations for the purchase of aircraft in exchange for financial advantage.

In India, on the other hand, Embraer signed a contract with the Singapore-based company Cleveden Limited, with the aim of making a payment of $5.76 million in return for the commercial representation services performed by Vipin Khanna. As the company was aware that the hiring of agents for military sales was prohibited in India, it sought to ensure the concealment of the contract signed with Khanna, recording that the negotiations would be for a sale made to a European customer.

The payment of bribes to members of the government of various countries, the concealment of the origin and nature of the payments made and the final recipients of the representation contracts signed, as well as the false records, were made with the intention of ensuring that the payments would not be blocked by Embraer's internal controls, since there was an internal policy that prohibited the signing of representation contracts after the conclusion of the main business.

Embraer entered into a Conduct Adjustment Agreement ("*CAA*") with the Federal Public Prosecutor's Office and the Securities and Exchange Commission due to the involvement of its directors in the practices of transnational active corruption and money laundering. According to the state bodies, in view of the collective protection of the economic order of public assets, the probity of the administration, the necessary repair of the damages caused, and the undoing of unjust enrichment, the company agreed to pay R$64,000,000.00 for the violation of the economic order and the principles and rules of transparency applicable to public companies.

The Company also committed to fully cooperate with the judicial and administrative processes, presenting all the information and evidence obtained from its internal

[11] U.S. Securities and Exchange Commission (SEC). (2016). *SEC Charges Embraer with FCPA Violations*. Litigation Release No. 23671.

investigations, such as a list of all employees, representatives, and contractors who could, in some way, collaborate with the elucidation of the facts. It is important to note that in the CAA the company's efforts with the extensive internal investigation carried out, as well as its collaboration with the ongoing processes and procedures, were recognised.

In the Sanctioning Administrative Process RJ 2015/1760, judged in 2018, against the company's directors, for violation of art. 154 of Law No. 6.404/1976 (Corporations Law),[12] the conduct of the administrators and the consequences of these on the reputational and financial aspects for the company were analysed, considering the payment of high fines and the commercial damage caused to Embraer. Director A was acquitted by the board due to the lack of evidence that could prove, beyond reasonable doubt, that he would have acted in the payment of undue advantages to international authorities.

Although the accused participated in meetings related to the sale of aircraft to the Dominican Republic, in his defence, he claimed that he trusted the information received from other areas of the company and that, given the trust he had in the professionals involved, he would have signed the documents. Director B, on the other hand, was sentenced to disqualification for a period of five years from serving as an administrator or fiscal advisor of public companies, as the evidence attached to the case demonstrated his active participation in the negotiations and decision-making related to the ways of signing contracts aimed at transferring the undue payments to members of foreign governments.

Embraer also entered into an agreement with the SEC committing to pay US$98.2 million, from which the amount eventually paid in the CAA celebrated with the Brazilian authorities would be deducted. In the understanding of the American body, the company would have violated the FCPA by using foreign authorities to achieve or facilitate the sale negotiations of its aircraft with the authorisation of its directors, who either knew of the irregularities or would have ignored the warnings (*red flags*) that indicated the high probability that the commercial representation contracts were, in fact, related to the payment of bribes.

For the SEC, Embraer's internal controls failed mainly due to (i) the non-existence of documents that could corroborate the contracts signed with companies that did not

---

[12] "*Art. 154 - The administrator must exercise the powers that the law and the statute confer upon him to achieve the ends and in the interest of the company, satisfying the requirements of the public good and the social function of the company.*

§ 1º The administrator elected by a group or class of shareholders has, towards the company, the same duties as the others, and cannot, even for the defence of the interests of those who elected him, fail in these duties. § 2° The administrator is prohibited from: (a) committing acts of generosity at the company's expense; (b) without prior authorisation from the general assembly or the board of directors, borrowing resources or assets from the company, or using, for his own benefit, of a company in which he has interest, or of third parties, its assets, services or credit; (c) receiving from third parties, without statutory authorisation or from the general assembly, any form of personal advantage, direct or indirect, due to the exercise of his position. § 3º The amounts received in violation of the provisions in clause c of § 2º belong to the company. § 4º The board of directors or the management can authorise the practice of reasonable gratuitous acts for the benefit of employees or the community in which the company participates, considering its social responsibilities".

perform activities related to aviation and (ii) the latent possibility of manipulating the accounting records. If those responsible had carried out the *due diligence* determined in the internal policies, they could have verified these clear inconsistencies and prevented the undue payments.

Finally, a DPA was signed with the DOJ also based on the violations perpetrated by the company to the FCPA and the irregularities in the accounting balances. With this body, Embraer committed to pay US$107.3 million and to hire an external and independent monitor to verify the fulfilment of the duties to implement effective controls and procedures to prevent the recurrence of the committed illicit acts.

5.5 Madero Case

With the so-called "*Weak Meat Operation*" the alleged payment of bribes by various food companies to public servants of the Ministry of Agriculture, Livestock and Supply ("*Ministry of Agriculture*") was investigated. The particularity of the involvement of Madero Industry and Commerce S.A. ("*Madero*") is that representatives of this reported to the Federal Police the demands made by employees of the Ministry of Agriculture and, in the criminal sphere, the company even appeared as a witness to the accusations of the public servants for extortion.

However, when its conduct was analysed by the CGU, in the administrative responsibility process instituted by Ordinance No. 1.238, of May 11, 2018, the company was fined in the amount of R$442,690.00 for the payment of bribes to the federal servers it had previously denounced.

The understanding of the CGU was that the Anti-Corruption Law provides for the objective responsibility of companies and, even though Madero made the payments at the demand of the public servants, it would incur in the conduct provided for in article 5, paragraph I, of the said law for having *given* undue advantage, in cash and in kind. The exhaustion of the illicit conduct would have occurred with the non-cessation of the company's operations, a threat made by the employees, according to the information presented in the case files.

The fact that Madero made the payments for approximately two years was seen by the CGU as a failure in internal controls, in which there were insufficient integrity instruments that allowed the company's representatives to adopt appropriate behaviours, in this case, the non-payment of any undue advantage. In this case, the repeated practice of payments, carried out for more than two years, and the participation of the management team in approving the conduct were considered aggravating factors. As mitigating factors, the CGU considered the company's cooperation with the investigations, the spontaneous communication of the irregularity, and the absence of damages.

5.6 Petrobras Case

The Petrobras case demonstrates the significant internal changes that can occur in a company after involvement in a large-scale scandal. In summary, the corporation had an *Executive Board* responsible for making decisions related to the company's objectives, strategies, and guidelines. In terms of hierarchy, this Executive Committee answered only to the *Board of Directors*. The absence of established internal policies for payment approval allowed the direction of undue amounts to company employees, politicians, and political parties.

According to the investigations carried out by the DOJ, senior Petrobras employees received bribes to favour the choice or even suspend the need for tenders. In preliminary meetings, it was usually explained that to secure certain contracts, it would be necessary to pay undue amounts to political parties. In fact, some contracts were signed precisely for this purpose.[13]

Although not all executives were linked to bribe payments, some were accused of deliberately failing to implement internal controls that could have prevented or at least raised alerts for many of the investigated conduct. Other employees were held accountable for the falsification of accounting documents presented to American authorities.

It is estimated that the improper conducts were practiced between the years 2004 and 2012 and that the bribes usually involved about 3% of the contract value. In the NPA signed with the DOJ, two major projects of the corporation were highlighted: (i) the Abreu e Lima Refinery, which involved more than 300 projects and 900 amendments, in which there was a conspiracy between contractors and suppliers with the aim of favouring the payment of millions of reais in bribes and (ii) the Rio de Janeiro Petrochemical Complex, in which tenders were waived and the direction of contracts to certain companies that had already agreed with the necessary payment of bribes as part of the agreement.

In summary, the DOJ understood that there was the instrumentalisation of the company, with the knowledge of its executives, through the direction of tenders, prior agreements for bribe payments that would grant contracts to companies that were not the most qualified, direct hires, and falsifications of the company's accounting information.

The internal problems of Petrobras, however, gave rise to one of the most complex internal control systems. If before the governance structures allowed the discretionary action of executives, the current model has completely changed this reality. Among the measures implemented, the areas of *compliance* and corporate governance were restructured.

All those involved in the pointed irregularities were dismissed from the company and, mainly, the most important deliberative bodies were remodelled. A new division was created for matters related to *compliance* and corporate governance, with a significant reduction in the cases of individual decisions (*four eyes approval policy*); the

[13] U.S. Department of Justice (DOJ). (2018). *Petróleo Brasileiro S.A.—Petrobras agrees to pay more than $850 million for FCPA violations.*

Ombudsman department was restructured; new procedures for hiring and promoting employees were established; improvements in anti-corruption training and the development of certifications for those who hold high positions; the creation of an Ethics Committee; the establishment of disciplinary measures and the risk-based analysis strategy for hiring third parties. With its new structure, the company sought to ensure the executives' commitment to the importance of internal controls and determined that its policies will be, at least, annually revisited.

Although the DOJ highlighted the fact that the company did not voluntarily disclose its irregularities, the relevant action in the investigations conducted was considered for the reduction of the sanction applied. According to the American agency, Petrobras cooperated extensively by instantly sharing the information discovered internally, facilitating the availability of interviews with foreign witnesses, collecting, organising, and analysing the evidence, as well as translating all relevant documents.

The sanctions applied to Petrobras were quite significant: a *cease-and-desist* procedure was applied with the SEC; an agreement was signed in a *class action* worth US$2.95 billion, to which was added the payment of a fine of US$853,200,000. Considering the ongoing processes in Brazil, the DOJ understood the absence of the need for the appointment of an independent monitor to follow the company's internal restructuring.

References

Barbosa PAR, Olivé JCF (2019) Compliance, Derecho Penal Corporativo y Buena Gobernanza Empresarial. Tirant lo Blanch, Bogotá

Peston R (2012) Are some banks too big to jail? BBC, 17 Dec

Steinberg RM (2012) The Game Changes: 10 Essential Elements for Truly Effective Compliance Programs

Taibbi M (2012) Outrageous HSBC Settlement Proves the Drug War is a Joke. Rolling Stone, 13 Dec

